ECUMENICAL STUDIES IN HISTORY

No. 6

ECUMENICAL DIALOGUE IN EUROPE

The Ecumenical Conversations at Les Dombes
(1937–1955) inspired by the Abbé Couturier

Introduced by

PATRICK C. RODGER

*Formerly Faith and Order Secretary,
World Council of Churches*

LUTTERWORTH PRESS

LONDON

ECUMENICAL STUDIES IN HISTORY

The purpose of this series is to examine afresh problems of Church History and to do this for the sake of Church Unity. The subjects are drawn from many periods, places and communions. Their unity lies not in a common outlook of the writers, nor in a common method of treatment. It lies solely in the aim of, in one way or another, directly or indirectly, furthering the unity of the Church. The contributors are no less diverse than the subjects, and represent many Churches, nations and races.

General Editors

CONTENTS

PREFACE TO THE ENGLISH EDITION (Patrick C. Rodger)   *page* 5

INTRODUCTION (René Beaupère)   8

I. HISTORY OF THE INTER-CONFESSIONAL GROUP OF LES DOMBES   11
   (Maurice Villain)

II. WHAT ECUMENICITY MEANS FOR US (Jean Bosc)   26

III. COMMENTARY ON THE THESES (J. de Baciocchi)   35

IV. THE THESES   52

V. CONCLUSION
   A PROTESTANT POINT OF VIEW (Henry Bruston)   62
   A CATHOLIC POINT OF VIEW (Gustave Martelet)   71

The Rev. Patrick C. Rodger is Vice-Provost of St. Mary's Cathedral, Edinburgh, and was formerly Faith and Order Secretary, World Council of Churches.

Fr. René Beaupère, O.P., is at the ecumenical centre St-Irénée at Lyon, and spends much of his time leading ecumenical pilgrimages to Palestine and Asia Minor. He is also editor of *Lumière et Vie*.

Fr. Maurice Villain, S.M., is one of the close disciples and the biographer of the late Abbé Couturier. He is an ecumenical "free lance" in Paris.

Professor Jean Bosc, Reformed Church of France, is Professor of Dogmatics, Faculté de Théologie de Paris.

Fr. J. de Baciocchi, S.M., is a professor at the Marist School in Lyon.

Fr. Gustave Martelet, S.J., is a professor at the Jesuit School of Fourvière, Lyon.

Pastor Henry Bruston is minister of the Lutheran Church at Lyon.

This book originally appeared as *Dialogue Oecumenique, Les recontres oecumeniques des Dombes, Verbum Caro*, No. 70, published by Les Presses de Taizé, France. The English translation has been made by W. Fletcher Fleet.

LUTTERWORTH PRESS
4 BOUVERIE STREET, LONDON, E.C.4

JOHN KNOX PRESS
RICHMOND, VIRGINIA, U.S.A.

Les Dombes is a Trappist monastery near Lyon.
Presinge is near Geneva.
Taizé, the Community of Taizé, near Cluny, Burgundy.
Cormatin is near Taizé.

*Printed in Great Britain by
Latimer Trend & Co Ltd, Plymouth*

PREFACE TO THE ENGLISH EDITION

To THE COMMON reader in the British Isles and the U.S.A., the mention of relations between Roman Catholics and Protestants in France probably conjures up pictures of the Massacre of St. Bartholomew's Day or of the Revocation of the Edict of Nantes, with perhaps some undertones of the bitter controversies of more recent times over Church schools and their relation to the State.

It is only a minority (though surely a growing minority) among us who are aware of the degree to which the exigencies of the twentieth century—the sufferings of two wars, companionship in the Resistance Movement and in succour to Algeria, but above all the common task of evangelism in a France as deeply secularized as England—have brought the two groups, the large and the small, out of the era of mutual hostility into some kind of fraternal relationship with each other.

It is an honour for one who has lived for several years on the fringe of this conversation, both in France and in French-speaking Switzerland, and has enjoyed the friendship of a number of the participants from both sides, to introduce this record of the inter-confessional group of Dombes, a record which testifies to a depth and seriousness of Catholic-Protestant conversation to which we in Britain and America (in our very different church situations) have rarely attained as yet.

The theological findings of this group have been well placed in their historical and personal context by Father René Beaupère and Father Maurice Villain, so that there is no need to try to steal their thunder in this respect. But British and American readers will surely be struck by certain qualities in this small book, which they may assess as "typically French": the lucidity and concentration of its contents, the use of ecumenical theses to enshrine agreements (and note the restraint whereby no theses are attempted when agreement cannot be reached, but difficulties are frankly expounded, as in the meeting of 1961), the understanding of the difference between an agreement and a mere compromise, the intelligent avoidance of traditionally explosive terms.

Perhaps, above all, we may feel drawn to that close connection between prayer and thought—"spirituality and theological reflection", as our French brethren would describe them—which has marked the history of this group from its earliest days before the Second World War, when such ecumenical encounter was indeed an adventure, risking censure and misunderstanding by the main body of both Churches concerned. Father Villain bears record of the spiritual influence of the Abbé Paul Couturier, who played a prominent part in the group until his death in 1953, and we may well see in these small meetings at Les Dombes, Taizé and Presinge—in French or Swiss, Catholic or Protestant, settings—a kind of first-fruits of that tremendous expansion of prayer and study in the service of Christian unity which all our Churches are experiencing today.

Since Pope John XXIII convoked the Second Vatican Council, and especially since the Council approved the decree on Ecumenism by an overwhelming majority in November 1964, encounters such as this book describes are being more and more urgently required, and we often realize how extremely unprepared and ill-equipped we are, Roman Catholics and others, to speak knowledgeably and constructively with each other.

We may therefore be grateful both for the prudence of the *groupe des Dombes* in waiting until there was a certain ripeness in their work over a period of twenty-five years, so that the reader may trace its progress and see how much has depended upon personal trust and friendship and upon deep ecumenical honesty in dialogue; and also for the decision to publish this "interim report"—for they intend, of course, to continue their meetings and indeed to enlarge them, since it is hoped to include Orthodox participants from now on—at a time when other groups in other countries may profit most opportunely from their experience.

In his contribution Professor Jean Bosc writes: "For us, ecumenism is a vocation and a command. We may not therefore conceive of it simply as the undertaking of a privileged circle of particular competence, but as a method of waiting and searching, lived always within the fellowship of the Church."

It is in this large spirit that the *groupe des Dombes* have pursued their way quietly for a generation, and those English readers who have taken part in similar groups, or who are just at the beginning of that road, will surely be encouraged by the way in which God has blessed that group and brought it, in surprising measure, to a common mind in Jesus Christ. They may also reflect that a greater degree of ecumenical contact across the Channel (including that between French and British Roman Catholics, and between French and British Protestants), and also across the Atlantic, could be sought with profit.

PATRICK C. RODGER

INTRODUCTION TO THE FRENCH EDITION

IN 1963, THE year which marked the tenth anniversary of the death of Father Couturier, the inter-confessional group of Les Dombes held a special session. Several members, who had joined the group in recent years, were desirous of obtaining fuller information not only about the history of this pioneer group, but about its spiritual life, its outlook and the results it had already achieved. All these members, too, felt the need of some kind of "retreat" to sum up what had already been gained and to think together about the future. Besides, in 1953, some months after the loss of Father Couturier, the normal series of theological conversations had already been interspersed with days of spiritual meditation.

It was during this gathering, held at the Trappist Monastery of Les Dombes, near Lyon, that the decision was reached to make public the "theses" which, since 1956, the group was in the habit of drawing up at the end of each of these gatherings to summarize the points of agreement and disagreement. The demand for such a publication had often been made. Up to this date the members had refused to meet this request, looking upon the theses rather as a kind of memorandum for the use of the members of the group, which would mark off the ground which had been covered and so save the members from going round and round, from bringing up the same problems for discussion, and from reopening subjects which could be considered closed. It was in a quite spontaneous way that, in 1956, the idea arose of expressing in writing the harmony which to all who had taken part seemed both outstanding and unexpected.

What kept the members of the Les Dombes group from making the results of their work widely known before this was not, we can be quite sure, any thought that there was anything discreditable or underhand about what they had been doing. Every year the report was drawn up by a select committee with the utmost care and submitted, before the end of the session, for the approval of those who had taken part. The reticence which was observed sprang really from the feeling that "theses", even more than texts, if they are torn up from the soil in which they have taken root and from which their vitality derives, run the risk of seeming either debatable or unimportant. It is possible, indeed, that those who constituted the group at Les Dombes—who form for the most part a group whose personnel hardly changes—invest these productions with a certain "aura" which derives from the conversations in which they have taken part and which is largely lost in cold print.

It is for this very reason that, as we seek to pass on to the readers something of this spiritual and theological wealth stored up by the Les Dombes group, we shall not content ourselves with setting out the "theses" baldly. Here they are, then, but inserted in their living context.

You will first be able to read the already considerable history of the group, as it is related by Father M. Villain. After this, Professor J. Bosc will attempt to draw up a full balance-sheet of the researches and thinking carried out in the group. Then Father J. de Baciocchi will recall the theological and dogmatic progress of the group from 1956 to 1963. This will lead on to the reading of the "theses", which are followed, not by a general bibliography of the subjects dealt with, but by a list of articles read to the group and later published in various reviews, especially in *Verbum Caro*. It must be borne in mind that this list includes only a portion of the important material which has been gathered together over the years, and that it would be advisable to follow up the reading of these lectures by other articles, even by published works of the members of the group. In these will be found, indeed, many indications of the fruit which our inter-confessional conversations have borne. The report which we present ends with two critical articles from Pastor H. Bruston and Father G. Martelet, who, after re-reading the theses in their entirety, pass their judgment on their soundness and their worth.

When one reads this collection, one will become aware of the principles which have characterized our work. We should like to call attention to one of these principles which is touched on only in passing in the articles but which profoundly affected the methods which were used, namely the composition of the group. From the confessional angle it is composed of Catholics and Reformed. Friends from the Lutheran, Anglican and Orthodox communions participated only occasionally in our gatherings. It is hardly necessary to say that this does not imply any unbrotherly exclusiveness or a failure to understand the universal character of ecumenical problems. The justification of this limitation is to be found rather in the existence of other groups engaged in such research but whose terms of reference are different. Has this voluntary limitation led to an impoverishment? It certainly would have done so had there been no link between the Les Dombes group and other inter-confessional teams. This is one of the aims of this publication. But in fact it seems to us that, in the matters under discussion between the Calvinist Reformed and the Roman Catholic communions, the theologians whose labours we are publishing, have reached, thanks to their specialization and the scriptural method which it makes possible, a keenness of perception and a precision which are rarely found elsewhere.

Walking together step by step—and often, alas, taking very short steps—they have set up landmarks which seem really enduring. Convinced, however, that they have cleared only a tiny part of the ground, they offer confidently to the theologians of all the Churches the fruits of their labours, hoping that they will be of use in further researches.

Often, at large ecumenical assemblies, one feels a certain disillusionment—we experienced this at times at the World Conference on Faith and Order at Montreal in July 1963. Delegates who are newly appointed tear to pieces the reports which have been presented to them and claim the right to reconstruct, in a few hours, theological studies which have involved two, five or even ten years of work in small specialist committees. We only hope that the "theses" of the Les Dombes group will not be too severely handled, but that readers will help by their constructive criticisms to further the work of the group, for what follows in this book is not a balance sheet but rather a milestone on a road which is still to be followed in the joyful hope of reaching unity.

RENÉ BEAUPÈRE, O.P.

I

HISTORY OF THE INTER-CONFESSIONAL GROUP OF LES DOMBES

One sows and another reaps. (John 4: 37)

THE FOUNDATIONS

The inter-confessional group of Les Dombes was founded by Father Paul Couturier in 1937. This pioneer of spiritual ecumenicity was also a man of wide contacts, a precursor of doctrinal ecumenicity, all of whose work bore the hallmark of experience.

Father Couturier had longed for this group at the outset of his ecumenical work, between 1932 and 1935, when he was still in the exploratory period, but at that time it was not easy to find a positive response from Reformed ministers.

I have already recounted in his biography the three stages of his contacts.[1] First with the Orthodox hierarchy: twelve years of relief work among the Russian refugees of the Lyon area opened up the way. A meeting with the Metropolitan Eulogius and a letter written by the latter (1934) were the starting-point for the leading article in the *Revue apologétique* (December 1935) which remained the charter for the "Week of Prayer". Soon afterwards contacts were established with the Anglicans: correspondence with Nashdom and other religious communities, visits to Lyon, Ars and Annecy of a number of prominent Anglicans; visits by Father Couturier to England in 1937 and 1938. On the second itinerary he was received by the Archbishops of Canterbury and York and made contact with numerous religious communities.

The relations with the Reformed Church began only later. These were also the outcome of the article referred to and were accepted in principle by the Synod of Agen in 1936. This Synod called upon the Reformed Churches in France to join in the prayers for Unity which were being offered at Lyon. Nevertheless, the first of these contacts

[1] *L'abbé Paul Couturier, apôtre de l'Unité chrétienne*, M. Villain, Paris, 1957, pp. 67 ff.

with Pastor Durand-Granier, in the presence of Dr. J. de Rougemont and Father H. Monchanin, was marked by a certain reticence. The Pastor had agreed to bring Father Couturier's plea before the Synod with Pastor A.-N. Bertrand of Paris as spokesman, but the very next day he wrote him a long letter which was not only reserved in tone, but which expressed outright disapproval of the ideas which Father Couturier had expressed and which he thought were in opposition to the doctrine and action of the Catholic Church. If the latter, said the pastor, had kept strictly aloof from the Stockholm and Lausanne conferences, it was proof that conversations with her were impossible. He had not grasped the level of complete surrender to God which marked his visitor's position. In any case, it was Pastor V. Rivet, the chairman of the Consistory of the Lyon district, who was the first to understand the real depth of the enterprise, which went far beyond classical apologetics. He was the first, at Lyon, to accept the hand which the Catholic priest held out to him. The way was open (January 1937). The same year the inter-confessional group came into being on the German-Swiss side through the offices of Father Laurent Remillieux, vicar of Notre-Dame Saint-Alban.

Before proceeding further, I must record the name of the friend, protector and patron of Father Couturier, the man without whose help the ecumenical work of Les Dombes would not have succeeded: Victor Carlhian (died 1959). An epitaph written by Jean Guitton will help us to assess this original and tireless figure.

> I write on the invisible monument, as on the Tomb of Archimedes, certain claims:
> Mathematician, physicist, logician, philosopher;
> Architect, designer, builder;
> Manager, printer, editor, writer and even stylist;
> Manufacturer, craftsman, artisan;
> *Ish Elohim*, as M. Pouget said, "man of God";
> Citizen, democrat, good neighbour, patriot, European;
> Ascetic, mystic, poor yet bountiful;
> Husband , brother, father, grandfather, and so very much the friend of his friends in their wide disparities;
> Hidden, unknown, *occultus in mundo*.

From 1920 to 1932, Victor Carlhian had taught Father Couturier a great deal in the conversations which they held during vacations on the estate of Saint-Ours (Isère). Fifteen years earlier, he had been the leading spirit in the *Sillon Lyonnais* and was still a Leftist. He passed on to

Father Couturier, who was from the extreme Right, his *Weltan-schauung* which was no less than a Christian and prophetic vision of the modern world. He directed his attention to Bergson, Chevalier, Laberthonnière, Teilhard de Chardin, with the flair of the true critic who can guess which men and which books will make history. But later, on the subject of ecumenicity, he was the humble pupil of his former pupil and his *salon*, from being a centre of scientific and philosophical activity, became an ecumenical *salon*. My own intro-duction into the ecumenical movement at Lyon was made even more pleasant by the dinners which members of different religious com-munions shared at the Quai de Bondy.

Alongside Victor Carlhian, mention must be made of four priests who, with Father Couturier and soon afterwards with myself, were to form the little Catholic group which offered a welcome to our Pro-testant brethren.

Father Laurent Remillieux, vicar of Notre-Dame Saint-Alban, "the little priest of a suburban parish who was able to overcome money and liberate the Church",[1] forerunner of the parochial revival, craftsman of peace and of Franco-German reconciliation, was endowed in addi-tion with an ecumenical passion. His wide contacts were at the dis-posal of the prophet. It was, indeed, he who brought to Father Couturier the first two recruits from German-speaking Switzerland: Pastor B. Zwicky of Herzogenbuchsee (Argovie) and Pastor R. Bäumlin of Erlenbach (Oberland) the founder of the Fraternité Saint-Jean in the Canton of Berne. On Sunday, May 30, 1937, he gathered a group of his parishioners and a number of Protestants on the lawn of Victor Carlhian's home at Saint-Alban. Father Couturier, Pastor Lucien Marchand (of Belfort) and Victor went there after their medita-tion: it was the Day of Pentecost for the Lyon ecumenical movement. In the same year was inaugurated the first gathering at Les Dombes, organized on the material side by Remillieux and on the spiritual side by Couturier.

M. Louis Richard, a Sulpician, was Professor of the Faculty of Theology. The *Sillon* had, long before this, brought him into contact with V. Carlhian. He recognized Couturier's prophetic significance and had been won over by his intuitions in ecclesiological matters; he was a wise and kindly critic of the Father, and he it was who issued the

[1] J. Folliet, *Le Père Remillieux, curé de Notre-Dame Saint-Alban, Chronique sociale de France et Centurion*, Paris, 1962. This journalistic portrait is rather feeble and abounds in errors in the four pages of ch. III on "the Apostle of Christian Unity".

"passport" to the "Copernican revolution" which spiritual ecumenicity represents in the Church. He was one of the most generally appreciated lecturers in the Les Dombes group. Certain of his studies published in the *Revue Apologétique* and in the *Nouvelle Revue Théologique* are reckoned among the first ecumenical publications of real value.

Father Joseph Chaîne, also a professor in the Faculty of Theology, has not left any published work in the ecumenical field, but his conversation was greatly appreciated by his Protestant brethren. A good, simple, down-to-earth man, he possessed a direct and realistic way of speaking of the Bible; he referred everything to the Book, even political happenings. May I add that his exegetical audacity sometimes frightened our naturally conservative German friends.

Father Monchanin was the most genial and the most widely cultured of the early helpers. In contact with Victor Carlhian since his ordination and a regular participator in the Saint-Ours conversations, his host recounted that together they had covered the whole domain of human effort (action, thought, art, love, religious experience) and paid a most moving tribute to Father Monchanin after his death.[1] Monchanin was haunted by the words in the prayer of Jesus "that the world may believe". From the time when he left the seminary, he glimpsed great bridges linking Christianity with Judaism, Islam, Hinduism and Buddhism, and he dreamed of being the architect. His whole life was lived out on the highest ecumenical level.

I am talking now only of the dead—the foundation-stones of our group. From among those still alive, I add two names. Father Chaillet, S.J., Professor of Ecclesiology at the Scholasticat de Fourvière, shared with us his work on J.-A. Moehler, pioneer of ecumenicity in Germany in the 1830's. According to Moehler the comparative study of the credal statements or confessions of faith of the different Christian groups supplies the first solid ground on which inter-confessional conversations can be built. But one must also go beyond these statements and try to grasp from within the secret of religious behaviour, belief put into practice and then one will recognize, so to speak, out of one's own experience the mystical foundation of the union of Christians in Christ. One was conscious of the beginnings of the method which was to become our own. Father Chaillet left us at the outbreak of the war and, after a valiant career in the Resistance, became manager of *Témoignage Chrétien*.

[1] Carlhian, *Souvenirs de mes dialogues avec l'abbé Monchanin*, in *L'abbé Jules Monchanin*, Casterman, Paris, 1960, pp. 41–49.

Father de Lubac, too, came once or twice to talk to us about "Tradition". In 1938 he published his *Catholicisme*,[1] a masterpiece which might be described as pre-ecumenical; whilst his aim is not primarily ecumenical, his reliance upon patristic sources, his approach to theological problems from angles familiar to Eastern Orthodoxy (those of the Greek Fathers, so near to the Bible and more concerned with contemplation of the mysteries than with scholastic systems), was a marvellous introduction to our conversations.

As I have said, our first Protestant colleagues were pastors from German-speaking Switzerland. They will, I am sure, forgive me if I am less explicit about their part in our work, as for twenty years they have joined us only on rare occasions.

One of them is dead, Peter Barth, brother of Karl, editor of the Latin text of *Christian Institutes*. He was a first-rate theologian. His presence called forth a letter from his illustrious brother who, at that time, was hardly enthusiastic in the ecumenical cause.

Pastor Richard Bäumlin made a great impression by his strong religious personality. Rather pietistic by nature, he showed a deep interest in dogmatic problems but, to his great regret, he could not express himself fluently in French. A thorough-going liturgist, aesthete and musician, he had brought about a spiritual transformation in his parish of Erlenbach, where twice, in 1938 and 1942, our group received an exceptionally warm welcome. Later, as Chaplain to the Deaconesses College at Berne, his gifts as spiritual director were recognized.

Pastor Berthold Zwicky exercised (and still does) his ministry at Herzogenbuchsee, in the canton of Argovie, to which work he added a military chaplaincy and, with Pastor Bäumlin, was the moving spirit in the Fraternité oecuménique of Saint-Jean.

Professor Otto-Eric Strasser, who was bi-lingual, was at that time minister of the church of La Paix, one of the most important parishes in Berne and at the same time Professor at the universities of Berne and Neuchâtel. He has written a thesis, which has won high praise, on the theological thought of Wolfgang Capiton.[2]

Pastors Heinrich Münger and Karl Huber were at the time assigned to country pastorates, but were talented classicists and Hebraists. The former, a citizen of Berne, struck me in his home surroundings as being like a man of the eighteenth century, able to improvise on the piano in the style of Mozart or Handel. These two inseparable friends brought into our group a note of gentle piety and frank gaiety.

[1] Le Cerf, Paris (Coll. *Unam Sanctam*, 3).   [2] Neuchâtel, 1938.

I have still to mention one of our colleagues of the early days, Pastor Lucien Marchand, of Belfort, the only Lutheran among us. He had undertaken, with M. Richard, an exposition of the Council of Trent and of the Augsburg Confession with the intention of finding a basis of agreement on the doctrine of justification. We all know how much progress has since been made along this line.

THE FIRST SERIES OF MEETINGS (1937-42)

1. *The setting and the programmes*

The setting of our meetings alternated between the Trappist Monastery of Les Dombes (about 40 kilometres from Lyon) and the presbytery of Erlenbach (Bernese Oberland). At Erlenbach we were accorded a family welcome in a magnificent countryside, the valley of Simmenthal at the foot of the Stockhorn and the Niesen. Notified of our coming, the whole village turned out to greet us. At Les Dombes we revelled in a monastic peace, surrounded by the gentle sounds of the plain, and we knew that the souls of our silent hosts were lifted to God in fervent prayer for the success of our talks. Had it not been for the war, we should have met twice each year; as it was, we were at Les Dombes in 1937, 1938, 1939 and 1942: at Erlenbach in 1938 and 1942.

The first gathering, at Les Dombes, was introduced by Father Remillieux as follows:

> This is how we shall spend our time during these three days: in the morning, after divine service, conversation. In the afternoon: two conversations. These very intimate conversations, interrupted by times for silence, for prayer and for personal intercourse, will give us the opportunity to unbend in the unity of prayer which we shall create.
>
> These are the suggested topics:
>
> Father Richard will introduce a conversation on the "Redemptive Act of Christ: The Last Supper and the Mass"; Father Monchanin on "The Mystical Body"; Father Couturier on "Questions Relating to Unity". I shall bring forward the subject of "Unity in our prayers, the Canon of the Mass and the prayers at the Lord's Supper".
>
> These are only suggestions. Our conversations will be fraternal, everyone will be free to put forward his own views, ideas and wishes on the proposed topics and on a host of cognate subjects.

The second gathering, at Erlenbach in 1938, was more formal, for at the outset the French priests were welcomed at the Federal Palace of Berne by the Minister for Religious Affairs, M. Dürrenmatt, well known for his desire to promote understanding between Catholics and Protestants.

The programme included widely diverse topics with no over-all plan. The impression is gained that each contributor brought what he had already prepared for some other occasion. In fact we were seeking to understand each other. It is vital, when setting out on such ventures, to sound the depths of each other's minds by choosing broad subjects. We sought to avoid points of friction, but these inevitably occurred. The themes, a rather miscellaneous collection, were:

"The Knowledge of God according to Nature and Revelation" (P. Barth), "The Holy Scripture in the Life of the Protestant Christian" (a Protestant), "The Sacramental Life in the Soul of the Catholic Christian" (a Catholic), "Salvation in Christ" (a Protestant), "The Idea of Redemption" (a Catholic), "The Pastoral Office of the Minister" (a Protestant).

The third meeting (Les Dombes, 1939) approached with some diffidence the theme of the Church: "The Origin of the Church; the Church on the March; the Church and her Consummation." This was the period when Father Chaillet edited the symposium *The Church is One*.[1]

The fourth, in the middle of the war (Erlenbach, 1942) dealt with spirituality, but again in a rather haphazard manner: "The Divine Office of the Catholic Church" (M. Villain), "The Spirituality of the French School" (L. Richard), "Spirituality of Friendship Groups in the University" (J. Chaîne), "Spirituality of the Pastoral Ministry" (R. Bäumlin), "Spirituality of Reform" (O. Strasser), "Theology of Spirituality" (G. Deluz).

2. *An atmosphere of prayer*

This paragraph ought to be written with a greater intensity than I can hope to achieve. The insistence of Father Couturier was, in this matter, decisive. His very presence, along with Bäumlin and Remillieux, all men of truly spiritual nature, created this atmosphere, and, from the moment of the inaugural gathering, we felt ourselves to be surrounded by prayer. Father Couturier loved free prayer as much as did our Protestant brethren; his prayers had an evident charismatic quality. R. Bäumlin composed long intercessions in German with a biblical ring to them, which he read in a French translation supplied by Father Remillieux.

[1] *L'Eglise est Une, hommage à Moehler*, Bloud et Gay, Paris, 1939.

The liturgy occupied a paramount place in our day. Each morning, a mass, in which all joined as far as was possible, was said in a gallery of the presbytery, adapted for this purpose, and at which the celebrant offered an extempore thanksgiving. For offices, we read the Psalms, because *L'Office Divin de l'Eglise Universelle*, a creation of *Eglise et Liturgie, a fortiori L'Office de Taizé*, which we use today, did not yet exist. Sometimes we would read Compline from the Roman breviary (in Latin). We gathered for evening service in the choir of the old village church (*januis clausis*) and on Sundays, in the gallery, we were present at the Lord's Supper celebrated by the pastor in a very elaborate form, a kind of *Deutsche Messe*, the order of which had been explained to us the previous night.

So, at the outset, each member entered at a deep level into the spiritual life of his separated brother, which is a factor of prime importance in ecumenical movements. It seems to me that we never again in later meetings reached this high degree of mutual understanding. Doubtless first impressions are ineffaceable. I am inclined to believe, however, that the spiritual tone has lowered; moreover, the permission to join in the Lord's Supper (even though granted for one occasion only and with extreme caution) was withdrawn, with the result that we no longer invite our Protestant brethren to attend Mass, except when they do so of their own accord at Les Dombes when the monks celebrate on our behalf a Mass for Unity.

3. *The Conversations*

The wording of the first programme made it quite clear that the conversations we held in the earlier years were marked by friendship, intimacy and restraint. Remillieux called them "conversations"; Couturier, "exchanges of views", never "debates" or "discussions". I emphasize the restraint which marked the conversations; one might almost find a hint of timidity, a certain reticence which sprang from the fear of hurting one's associates. This arose from our desire to understand the mentality of the "others" without books or master to teach us. This demanded numerous and detailed records, personal reflections on these records in order to draw up a coherent and articulated whole. Now that the initial "running-in" period is over and that we are perfectly equipped for our task, we no longer set ourselves problems of this nature and contact is immediate.

The result was a joyful experience of Christian love, Christian brotherhood at last discovered in all its freshness; my "separated" brother is first and foremost my "Christian" brother through his baptism; Christ died for him as He did for me; Christ loves him as He loves me and perhaps even more; Christ saves him as He saves me, only by a slightly different road. Twenty-five years ago such views, which today have become commonplace, were new, and whoever advanced them openly ran the risk of being accused of lukewarmness, which was certainly wide of the mark. On that account, we felt a burning desire to come to understand this brother completely, to make ourselves understood by him, to grasp together in a common effort the truth which is in Jesus Christ.

We needed this special grace at the beginning of our task to encourage us and to strengthen our wills to overcome the obstacles which cropped up all the time. On both sides we were in entire agreement that we could not rest content with this result, however comforting it might be to have formed amongst ourselves an enduring friendship. That being assured, we had now to find a way of ordered methodical conversation and to find this, too, without a guide.

A picture which was carried away from Erlenbach shows this stage clearly. One day, Father Chaîne, comparing our position with a crevasse between two walls of a glacier, said, "The crevasse does not go to the very bottom, for we all possess the common foundation: Jesus Christ." But how zealously we had to guard against illusion. However narrow the crevasse seemed to us at times, it still hid an abyss.

SECOND SERIES OF MEETINGS (1945–55)

A little while before the Second World War, Father Couturier decided to form a second inter-confessional "cell" which, for reasons of linguistic convenience, was to be recruited from French and French-speaking Swiss pastors. On the Protestant side, the leadership was entrusted to M. Jean de Saussure, who at that time occupied the pulpit of the Cathedral of St. Peter at Geneva. Professors of the Universities of Montpellier, Geneva, Lausanne, Neuchâtel, Paris and Strasbourg, pastors from Lyon, Paris, south-eastern France, brothers from the Taizé Community and (after the 1948 Amsterdam Assembly) members of the World Council of Churches staff responded to the appeal.

Father Couturier at first hoped that the two groups could work side by side with the co-operation of the same Catholic members. These were recruited from among the professors of the Faculty of Theology at Lyon, the Theological Colleges of Fourvière and Sainte-Foy, and from various French seminaries, from the religious orders and from the diocesan clergy. But these priests were overburdened with work and could not meet the requirements of two separate series of conversations. The compromise, since the ideal was unattainable, would have been to fuse these two groups, but this proved undesirable. Very soon, indeed, we realized that the exacting nature of the conversations to which we were committed demanded from each side as complete a homogeneity as possible. So, to our profound regret, our German friends, who were not entirely in harmony with their French or French-speaking Swiss colleagues, practically dropped out. We were distressed at this, especially those among us who had experienced the *charismata* of the first meetings, but circumstances were stronger than our most fervent desires.

From the moment when the second team was formed, the location of the centre to which the Protestants invited us changed: in turn it was at the "Abbey" of Presinge, secured for us by Pastor de Saussure, once each at Grandchamp and Taizé, and now it is at Cormatin, whilst the monastery of Les Dombes remains the Catholic base.

The following list refers to this second series of meetings up to 1955. Since then our sessions have been followed regularly by the issue of transactions.

1942 This series opened at Les Dombes in the middle of the war (September 28). The gathering was carefully prepared for at Geneva by Pastors J. de Saussure and J. de Senarclens, at Lyons by Father Couturier and myself. The subject: "Study of the Epistle to the Ephesians."

On the Protestant side, I call attention to the names of R. Chapal, Du Paquier, N. Ehrenström, Henriod, R. Paquier, R. de Pury, J. de Saussure, A. Schlemmer, A. de Weymarn. For the first time R. Schutz and M. Thurian came.

On the Catholic side: Chaîne, Gaudefroy (who almost succeeded in bringing Marcel Legaut), de Lubac, P. Couturier and M. Villain. A German friend, M. Paulus Lenz, a refugee in France since the rise of Nazism, was unable to be with us and handed his script to P. de Lubac.

The journey was not without incidents. On the station platform at Perrache, Pastor Cassalis and a Catholic from the Resistance waited for us, greeted Pastor de Pury and engaged him in a mysterious conversation in the railway carriage at the end of the corridor, while we kept watch. The conversation continued in the Café de Marlieux, after which the conspirators vanished.

1943 An attempt was made to form a third cell of a pastoral nature, with the French pastors of the Drôme and the Ardèche. I have in my records the correspondence exchanged between Pastors P. Courthial (of la Voulte-sur-Rhône) and Gennatas and Father Jean Clemence, S.J., on the subject of "Prayer". The meeting was never held.

1945 Fresh setback: over the matter of a retreat of a theological nature at X. . . . It was on this occasion that permission to attend *even once* the Lord's Supper was withheld from the Catholics. This refusal compelled us to suspend our projects.

1946–55 and since, no interruption:

1946 at Presinge: "Tradition".

1947 at Les Dombes: "The Church". These two meetings were followed by roneotyped reports edited by M. Thurian and myself. At that time we should not have been in a position to sign a joint statement.

1947 at Les Dombes: Again "The Church".

1948 at Grandchamp: "Prophecy"; "Mary".

1949 at Les Dombes: "Pastoral Teaching on the Sacraments".

1950 at Presinge: "The Sacraments".

1951 at Les Dombes: A journey to the United States prevented my attendance at this session where an effort was made "to understand the different views through historical and political events".

1952 at Les Dombes: "Merit"; "The Last Things"; "The Intercession of the Saints".

1953, the year in which Father Couturier died, we held a retreat at Taizé on the "Lord's Prayer".

1954 at Presinge: "Christ" (a study of the Definition of Chalcedon).

1955 at Les Dombes: "The Holy Spirit".

There was as yet no clear overall plan: a concern about ecclesiology dictated the choice; but the selection of subjects, year by year, sprang from a need which had been felt in carrying out the preceding programme. The subjects were linked rather by a kind of inward logic. From 1956 onwards, as will be seen in the studies which follow, we began to look for an organic plan, taking into account the important observation of the Lund Conference: that there is an intrinsic connection between Christology and ecclesiology.

The talks were ordinarily duplicated (the same subject was treated twice) so that we might understand more fully the two extremes of thought and appreciate more completely the vocabularies used. Today, this is no longer necessary, except in extraordinary circumstances when dealing with particularly difficult problems.

The conclusions were not drawn up jointly, as we have done since 1956; sometimes two parallel accounts were required (as in 1946 and 1947). However, we have long since passed the stage of debate and are well on the way towards an ecumenical theology. This is the final point with which I must deal.

TOWARDS A SYSTEM OF ECUMENICAL THEOLOGY

It is quite impossible for me to sum up the work accomplished during those first twenty years, as I have insufficient notes to guide me through this somewhat difficult terrain. One thing, however, is quite sure, namely, that we had very early on discerned the basis of an ecumenical method which is equally valid for both sides. And I venture to claim that we owe this—at least initially—to the driving force of Father Couturier.

Some superficial observers have failed to understand that our leader did not confine himself to "spiritual" ecumenicity, in which field he was the undisputed master, but that, in his view, spiritual ecumenicity inevitably led to "doctrinal" ecumenicity for which it supplied the necessary dynamic, so much so that both constituted an integral part of one method. This point was always clear to those who worked along with Father Couturier. I was driven to emphasize this rather strongly in the third edition of *Introduction à l'oecuménisme*,[1] being convinced that some of my Catholic critics had completely failed to grasp the inseparable connection between these two aspects. There is an abundance of material in the writings of Father Couturier to illustrate this inevitable transition from spirituality (or theology at prayer) to dialectic theology of an ecumenical character or, as he loved to say, from "Christophoria" to "Christophania". One is advised to consult the passages on *Theologie Priante* (p. 151), *Christophorie et Christophanie* (p. 148), *Problème et surproblème* (pp. 187–94), *Dynamisme et loyauté* in his book, *Oecuménisme spirituel*.[2] These texts belong respectively to the years 1943, 1941, 1944, 1945 and, although written twenty-five years

[1] Casterman, Paris, 1961.

[2] *Oecuménisme spirituel. Les écrits de l'abbé Paul Couturier, Présentation et commentaire de M. Villain, Préface de S. B. Maximos IV*, Casterman, Paris, 1962.

ago, should be considered in the light of the Second Vatican Council. A reading of these texts will prove beyond doubt that this great spiritually-minded man was profoundly versed in theological matters with a prophetic instinct which went far beyond the normal. Among notes which I made at the time are the following:

"In the exchanges of views (he preferred that expression to the word discussions), he most frequently remained silent, his face amazingly contemplative. When he did intervene to ask a question or to suggest some elucidation, he did so with an infinite delicacy. When clashes occurred, he lifted the debate to a higher level in search of a synthesis. The theological specialists at first sometimes protested, but upon reflection would often be amazed at the pertinence and the profundity of the interjection: Father Couturier, they would feel, had glimpsed, beyond the classic differences, even beyond the plain YES—NO, a hidden similarity, a common direction, a germ capable, God willing, of providing the first beginnings of an agreement. Is not the mark of the real 'theologian' the fact that he is illuminated by God to speak about the mysteries of God? Despite his natural boldness and the excitement which the ecumenical question stirred in him, he never ignored the solid facts of dogma: they remained present in his mind by a kind of instinct.

"His revered presence made a profound impression on everyone, for he radiated Christ. When, from time to time, voices rose and the exchange of views was in danger of turning into an acrimonious discussion, we knew that, if we merely looked at him, we could not go on in that way. The thought of mastering an opponent was quite untenable. He would interrupt quietly to suggest that we should seek the guidance of the Spirit in silent prayer and postpone the discussion to later. Once (at Grandchamp when he was absent) the speakers, who had been rather sharp, asked each other's pardon."

I confess that it was when I thought about this gift, which was intuitive rather than rational, that I conceived, in 1944, the idea of what might become, in the best sense of the term, an ecumenical theology. I therefore undertook the first attempt at turning what with Father Couturier was an encounter of souls and thoughts in prayer, an apprehension of rudimentary ideas, a following up of lines—into dogma. I realized that direct contact removed prejudices and unreal problems, set difficulties in their true perspective, corrected positions distorted in the classic controversy, lit up the meaning of the terms used; in short, prepared the way for a cordial and frank understanding, an outcome by no means insignificant. This method, which I sketched in 1944 and which was tried out from 1945 in our meetings of priests in the attempt to discover an ecumenical theology, was based entirely on the experience of the meetings we held in the early years, and filled in from year to year as the particular programmes were carried out.

This study, included in the fourth part of my *Introduction à l'oecuménisme* (chs. 3 & 4) need not be repeated here. I will content myself with giving the headings.

The method which emerged from our first attempts involved three stages (which I will describe from the Roman Catholic standpoint):

1. *To preserve, under all circumstances, all that is valid in the Protestant position.* Now, since we made a serious attempt to judge things from their point of view rather than our own, we know how many things of permanent validity are to be found in the Protestant position. The first 144 pages of Father Louis Bouyer's book, *Du Protestantisme à l'Eglise*, are the standard for us; they correspond, in the main, to the discovery we made in the Les Dombes group.

2. *Seek to expound our doctrine in a constructive, not a polemical, manner.* A polemical theology is full of inherent weaknesses.

3. *Proceed together to a synthesis.* This work cannot be begun before the question is faced which is vital to every conversation: the relation between *Scripture and Tradition.* There is a way of resolving this question which puts an end to all conversation: to say that there are *two sources,* the second of which *supplements* the former. There is another answer which allows conversations to proceed: to say that Scripture and Tradition are *two aspects* of the same source, Jesus Christ. When we affirm that Scripture contains all the truths necessary to salvation (as was always thought until the Council of Trent) and when we Catholics add that Scripture must be read through the eyes of the Church (the Church "aided" by the Spirit does not dominate "inspired" Scripture but rather serves it), we certainly do not resolve the whole difficulty (because for us Catholics the reading of the Bible is strictly "normative"), but at least an exchange of views is possible. For we can work together on the basis of the one common Scripture without going so far as to admit that *Scriptura sola* is the basis of faith. So we can go a long way towards meeting the demands of Professor F. J. Leenhardt who recognizes that there is a Catholic interpretation of Scripture which is, both exegetically and theologically, *authentic.* This admission seems very important in that it permits the conversations to go on, and with this

modest result we can be satisfied for a long time to come. It is modest, granted, but it is growing from year to year, and it has never occurred to us to rest on our achievements.

Thus, we do not strive to get the better of one another in debate: quite simply, we are building with the help of the Lord.

MAURICE VILLAIN, Paris.

II

WHAT ECUMENICITY MEANS FOR US:
STOCKTAKING, PRESENT TASKS AND METHODS

THE PURPOSE OF the study which has been assigned to me is, if I have understood it aright, to try to draw up a "balance-sheet" of the research and thought in which the Les Dombes group has been engaged for the past twenty years, and, as far as is possible, to sketch the fresh perspectives which open up for our work. It is in this context that we have to ask ourselves what ecumenicity means for us.

It is clear that two dangers threaten such an undertaking: one danger is that of falling into the error of useless repetition, battering on doors which are already wide open; ecumenicity is a domain which has long been familiar to all of us and this very familiarity might stand in the way of one whose conscience has been newly awakened to its claims. The other risk which faces me is that of presenting the facts in far too personal a manner, when the real issue is what ecumenicity means to the study group to which we belong and in terms of work actually accomplished. I am not confident of my ability to evade these two dangers. Perhaps, after all, it is best not to be obsessed by such dangers, whilst remaining fully aware that they do exist.

I. WHAT ECUMENICITY MEANS FOR US

We can put this in the form of a question: what have we learned together about ecumenicity during these years of study and conversation which have been for us so precious an experience? It seems to me that one may, at this stage, define the meaning of ecumenicity for us in three ways which are linked together and complementary.

A. *Ecumenicity meant in the first place and still means to us the awareness of a contradiction which we cannot refuse to face on the grounds that it has already been resolved.*

This contradiction is that of a divided Christian Church. The pre-ecumenical situation is characterized by a kind of passive acceptance, or even at times by an active justification, of this division. An anxious conviction of the truth in which men believe prevails, in extreme cases absolutely, over the concern for unity, and in the process the truth itself becomes distorted and deformed. Ecumenical awareness, on the contrary, comes into being, is established and grows from the moment when unity is acknowledged as one dimension of truth and when the division of the Church is recognized as a threat to the truth which the Church treasures.

All that has to be done is to reverse the order. For the awareness of the contradiction posed by the division of the Church is linked with the recognition that this division is overcome by the One Lord, Jesus Christ, in the work of reconciliation which He accomplished and in the promise of His coming in glory. It is because Jesus Christ is the One Lord that the division of His One Body is a contradiction: but because He is proclaimed once for all as the One Lord, because He still is and will for ever be the One Lord, the division of His Body is overcome.

In other words, it can be asserted that all our ecumenical activities have their source, their foundation and their goal in a "Christological concentration". It is because we are and desire to be Christians in the deepest sense of the word—clothed with Christ, grafted into Him—that we feel this contradiction; it is because our gaze is fixed on Christ that we know that we have overcome this division; and it is because this knowledge has been revealed to us in growing clarity and depth that we have felt an inward compulsion to face up to this contradiction.

Although it is too early yet to speak of a common theology, it is nevertheless clear that this "Christological concentration" which we share supplies a converging theological orientation. It is this same orientation which was accepted by the Faith and Order Commission of the World Council of Churches after the Lund Conference. We experienced something analogous to the plan for Conversations between Roman Catholics and Protestants.

The immediate consequence of this awareness and of this orientation is that certain extreme positions and certain dissident tendencies by which our Churches are threatened, each with its own particular temptations, are taboo among us. To give only one example, it seems to me an inevitable conclusion that a Catholic theologian cannot unilaterally dogmatize on the unity of the visible Church nor a Protestant theologian on liberty under the Word. Absolute freedom to express ideas of unity or of liberty can lead only to parallel closed systems. It is only in so far as these ideas are thought out in Christ that they have any truth and vitality. Mutual Christological convergence rules out unity or liberty as being myths or abstract principles and opens up the way to a genuine ecumenicity.

B. *Ecumenicity represents for us a theological discovery and a theological responsibility.*

Primarily this discovery is one which has been made by both sides, doubtless on the personal level, but it must always be borne in mind that, in the conversations, the members speak as representatives of their respective Churches. It is because of this that theological discovery has been based on the friendly and fraternal relations which have been formed between us. This discovery has been, and still is, undoubtedly slow; a long waiting period is needed if it is to be genuine and if it is to go down to the roots of the various attitudes and positions, but it is a real thing.

When I look at these matters from my point of view as a member of the Reformed Church of France, I believe that the main line in this discovery is the one which leads from scholastic dogmatism to the real profundities of dogma, from the systematic formulation and historic definitions of that dogma to the living truth which dogma seeks to embody. Perhaps, on the Catholic side, the corresponding journey is that which moves from the arid, external negativeness of Protestantism to the positive foundation on which the claim made by the Reformers rests.

It would doubtless be possible to present the facts in a rather different way, but essentially that is the road that ecumenicity has opened up to us, the road that it keeps on challenging us to make and remake, in a patient struggle against our closed minds, our prejudices and our instinctive conservatism. One of the most striking results of our ecumenical study has undoubtedly been—here and elsewhere—the discovery that the authority of Roman Catholic dogma was not to be mistaken for a literal belief in the formulas but required elucidation in a principle of interpretation which appeals to the sources and to the analogy of faith. Of course, we know that there are important sectors of Roman Catholicism where there is no clear awareness of this necessity for such an interpretation of Catholic doctrine, a necessity which Pope John XXIII expressed clearly on a very important occasion;[1] the realization of this was one of the decisive elements which enabled us and still

[1] In his opening address to the Second Vatican Council.

enables us to advance towards an inner understanding of the dogmas and of their roots. This in no sense implies that, on either side, we are thereby usually led to accept what formerly we rejected: but our adhesion or our rejection is expressed in a different tone, is based on other grounds; both adhesion and rejection take on a brotherly and spiritual gravity far more striking than we could have imagined.

To express it in another way, it seems to me that for us ecumenicity is a discovery in depth of the catholicity of the faith of the Christian Churches. Of course, we had been told often that we are Evangelical Catholics, as you are Roman Catholics. But the actual ecumenical experience has afforded us an ever-widening opportunity of measuring, in time, in space and in the deepest recesses of truth, the dimensions of this catholicity. As far as we Protestants are concerned, this ecumenical research has enabled us the better to understand how deeply our Protestant faith is rooted in a broad and living Catholic tradition; and I hope I may be allowed to voice my impression that, in these ecumenical exchanges, the interpretation placed by the Roman Catholics on the same catholicity has in some measure been stripped of unessentials or purified. Doubtless Catholics and Protestants still cherish what they feel to be authentic in their traditions, but with this great difference—from now on we shall always be able to discern through and beyond our emphases the mystery of catholicity.

This discovery, which beckons to ever new horizons, implies for us an ever-growing theological responsibility. For it opens our eyes to the immediate situation, the lack of understanding, the fanaticism which for so long has characterized the theologians and their theologies. This does not mean that they have neglected to seek the truth, but that they have so often sought it in a narrow, defensive way, without that freedom which alone can lead to the full light. Little by little, we are rediscovering this freedom which makes greater and greater demands upon us, namely that we should re-learn, in the liberty of the Spirit, how to think things afresh, how to talk to one another, how to seek together.

It is incumbent upon us to put into practice what we have learned about the relativity of theology, or more exactly that theology is the servant of the Word of God; ecumenicity is the school in which we learn humility. It is vital that we should advance towards the discovery or the reanimation of a language which will set us free from our conceptual prisons and provide us with a common medium for research. We must not weary of seeking to understand the deepest intentions in

C

the affirmations of our respective creeds. We must keep on returning together to the sources of our faith.

This is an arduous task, but full of immense promise.

C. *Ecumenicity is for us obedience and expectation on the ecclesiastical levels.*
The study and the work which ecumenicity implies for us are unthinkable except in the Church, with the Church and for the Church. We did not choose to launch into an ecumenical adventure; the ecumenical cause gripped us as a demand which had to be obeyed. From both sides we can reiterate, in a different situation and context, the claim of Luther at Worms: "We can do no other." Ecumenicity might at times seem to be a fashion, a craze or mere opportunism. For us it is a vocation and a command.

That is why it cannot be viewed as the enterprise of a privileged and competent circle, but as a hope and a quest realized within the communion of the Church. This fact shapes our effort in several ways:

1. This effort is inconceivable except in a profound and constant solidarity with our respective Churches; this is one aspect of the matter which has often been referred to, but there is nothing lost by emphasizing it again. For as an ecumenical theology comes into being and develops, so also the danger increases that the gulf between the specialists and the Christian rank and file might widen: it is not unimaginable that, alongside, beyond and above the Churches, there might be set up unawares an *ecclesiola* of ecumenists. Very special vigilance is necessary on this point.

2. This implies that, over and over again, we must remind ourselves of the difficulties and the obstacles which arise from the presence side by side of these Churches with their varying teachings. We must not let the fact that certain problems have been solved for us blind us to the actual tension which exists between these Churches. On the other hand, there are in our communities impetuous enthusiasms which have to be kept in check. In other words, ecumenicity demands, along with study and research, the slow task of instructing the Churches in the perspective of unity.

3. But the Church is not unified for her own sake: her presence on earth is linked with her mission. Unity is given and must be demonstrated so that the world may believe that the Father has sent the Son. A genuine ecumenical study cannot be developed without reference to the missionary dimension of the Church.

4. Above all, we must embody the theological contradiction, as well

as the theological research, in the prayer-life of the Church. Like every other theology, that which occupies our attention can never be an end in itself; it is part of the service of Christ; it goes hand in hand with all the other forms of this service and consequently is always directed and subjected to Christ. Its finality and its meaning are shown, given and sustained by prayer.

In short, for us ecumenicity is rooted in the unity, catholicity, apostolicity and holiness of the Church. That is also why we accept the vocation which it implies as a favour which is a source of unfailing joy,

II. THE PRESENT TASK

The present task follows inevitably the line along which we have already progressed and which has been defined above. It is clear that the further we advance, the more pronounced becomes the urgency and importance of this task. It is very remarkable, in this respect, that in recent years in our Churches there has been an urgent, definite and growing appeal to theology and the theologians, and this has often closely coincided with the progress of the ecumenical movement. In this domain one has only to think of the first session of the Vatican Council when a considerable number of bishops revealed an awareness of the ecumenical challenge, a questing spirit and an open mind. Similar signs are to be found in Protestantism. This phenomenon constitutes for us at the same time an answer to our prayers and a joyful obligation.

If we are to persevere in the same way, it cannot be, however, without a certain renewal. Up to now we have been chiefly preoccupied with facing the most vital and central questions which have to be settled between our Churches in the dogmatic field. We were assuredly right and we must keep these objectives before us; we have had enough experience to know how vital it is to the authenticity of our conversations that we should face squarely the fundamental doctrinal questions.

But I do not think, however, that we can stop there. We are well aware that if the major difficulties between us lie at the heart of doctrine, they are not only central and not only theological; they have repercussions on secondary doctrinal problems as well as in the area of spiritual life and piety.

It is fairly widely agreed today, for example, that there is a very close approximation of points of view on the doctrine of grace (justification, sanctification, etc.). But what importance can be given, then, to the practice of indulgences, to the belief in Purgatory, to the transfer of merit? We do not feel far from each other when we discuss the doctrine of the Eucharist as a sacrament. But what is the meaning of the practice of reserving the elements or adoring the Blessed Sacrament? The whole question of Mariology, which so far we have left aside, would have to be raised in the same way.

Thus there can be found, under various headings, a whole series of subsidiary questions which it would certainly have been wrong for us to study at the outset, but whose bearing is far too important for us to be able to go on ignoring them. I have chosen the examples which occur to me as a Protestant looking at Catholicism. On your side you will have to carry out a corresponding examination of Protestantism. I have the feeling that here we are facing a divergence of attitude, a difference of spiritual climates of supreme importance; we have often referred to it and O. Cullmann emphasized it on the occasion of the Vatican Council.[1]

You, Roman Catholics, still think of us as Christians or as communities who *lack* certain precious and important elements of the Christian faith. We are embarrassed by what seems to us *superfluous* in the doctrine and devotional life of Catholicism. You aim at comprehensiveness when you accept the fact that certain elements assumed by the Church are not always pure; our preoccupation is rather with proving the authenticity of beliefs and practices even if it means that we run the risk of impoverishing the life of our Church. It seems to me that the time has come when all this should be gone into thoroughly and when the idea of comprehensiveness, to which we both hold, even if with different connotations and requirements, should be examined. In my opinion this examination ought to be carried out along with a theological scrutiny of our respective liturgies, our forms of private devotion, our susceptibilities. Doubtless it is equally important to face, in a similar way, the question of ethics as it concerns our two confessions.

In short, without losing sight of the basic principles of our research, we must widen the ground so as to reach a more coherent, more practical and—one must hope—more constructive view of the matter. The results already achieved ought to enable us to do this effectively.

III. METHODS

When one comes to deal with the problem of methods, one is always somewhat embarrassed. One must never grow weary of em-

[1] Press Conferences, Nov. 23, 1962, published in *Foi et Vie*, 1963, No. 1; see pp. 59 f.

phasizing that in the final issue there are no methods, or at least that method must always be secondary. For what makes conversations and study fruitful is essentially the deep-seated attitude of each side towards the other, the will to understand, mutual patience, the disposition to listen, prayer together, a common movement back to the source. If one keeps that in mind it is quite possible to speak of a method, or at least of certain elements of a method. Our experiences enable me to indicate some possible lines:

1. It is essential that we should always seek, in a growing understanding of revelation, to penetrate the profoundest aspects of Christian truth, without being obstructed by the very rigid forms in which these aspects have been expressed in one tradition or the other. For example, the Roman Catholic definitions of the Infallibility of the Church, or the Protestant declaration concerning *sola scriptura*, cause a shock when they are looked at in their starkness. But they can lose their rigidity and become, not necessarily acceptable, but at least comprehensible, when one seeks to penetrate what they are really trying to express. This effort to sound the depths of the meaning of credal statements, if it is to be truly fruitful and valid, demands a constant recourse to the Scripture and the Fathers. On this point our experiences seem to me to be decisive and our method must be retained and even intensified.

2. In my opinion, the study of vocabulary and languages ought to occupy a very important place in our research; perhaps we have not given sufficient attention to this point. Ecumenical activity has made it clear that the vocabulary used by different Churches or theological schools and at various periods in history is frequently interpreted in an inadequate and erroneous way. This is the cause of opposing views which, at least in certain circumstances, were due to misunderstandings. We must follow a completely new course of semantic study and apply it to particular concepts and to biblical vocabulary.

3. From that point we must adhere to the custom we have adopted of saying together everything which we can say together. The publication of the theses to which we have devoted ourselves for many years is one of the most useful aspects of our work. Linguistic study would enable us to go even further than we have done in this field and especially to discover a language more common to all of us.

4. Ought we not to see to it that *all* the members of the Les Dombes group take a more active part in its work and study? It would be invaluable if, between the sessions, every member had the chance and

took the trouble to re-examine, to annotate and to comment on the texts which have been drawn up.

5. It would seem to me highly desirable that, at the point which we have reached, we should try to get to know, more intimately and in a more practical fashion, the life of our respective Churches. A regular supply of information about the life of these Churches, the trends which are developing, the problems which confront them, would be of priceless worth for our mutual understanding.

In short, what is required is both a deepening and a broadening of the work which has been undertaken in our group. The Vatican Council has, in some measure, put the stamp of its approval on the method which was followed and the work which was done in the preceding period. Now it is up to us to seek to exploit more fully what has already been accorded to us. Our gratitude for what we have seen and received can only be a spur to encourage us to go steadfastly ahead.

JEAN BOSC, Paris.

III

COMMENTARY ON THE THESES

THE IDEA OF setting forth the theses that we all unanimously accepted came to us during the session of 1956, when we joyfully discovered a truly unexpected proximity of views on the Christian doctrine of man, and especially on original sin. The joint theses which were the product of that year's meetings deal solely with this theme, although our conversation ranged also over the subject of Christ as "New Man" and the life of grace open to His disciples.[1]

The first thesis was added after the end of the meeting, by the Lyons team, which comprised at that time five pastors, three of whom had taken part in the conversations, and seven priests, of whom five had formerly taken part in the group study. The thesis establishes our awareness of original sin, which does not spring from abstract philosophical speculation, but from divine revelation, closely linked with the redemptive work of Christ:

"Our redemption in Jesus Christ makes clear to us that outside that redemption we are subject to the rule of sin."

In the subsequent theses you will notice the deliberate omission of technical terms used in current theology, and especially of the term NATURE. The discussion had indeed confirmed what was suspected at the outset, that for Catholics and Protestants (as for scholastic philosophy and modern thought in a different way) this term has different meanings.

"The conflicts in the 16th century sprang to a large degree from different concerns. Whereas in the expression 'human nature' the Catholic Church had

---

[1] The joint theses drawn up subsequently were never thought of as a *résumé* of all our doctrinal study, nor of everything that was said at the meeting which drew them up, nor even of everything on which agreement was reached during that meeting. They are just guide-posts marking the points of agreement which seemed the most original, the most critical or the most important, and which mark a step forward in our conversations, or bases to hold for future advances.

in mind the ontological status of man, the Reformers, inspired by their essentially soteriological concern, took it to include the original relationship of man with God."

The perspective of the theses on the state of sin is a perspective of *personal relations* between God and men and between men themselves. This is the reason for the use of such ideas as the broken covenant, state of revolt, rejected vocation, spiritual solidarity between men, etc. On the other hand, in line with the group's traditional method, we have used biblical ideas: sin, covenant, eternal life, death, salvation, etc. Finally, various realities dependent on "nature" in the scholastic sense of the word have been referred to with the help of modern ideas which are almost, if not entirely, non-technical: aspirations, values, free will, ambiguity. . . .

The theses in this first series which are still to be examined may be divided into three groups, of two, three and three, with Thesis 10 as the conclusion.

Theses 2 and 3 express the fundamental nature of our state of sin: on this matter complete unanimity was reached at once.

2. *"The state of sin lies at the root of all our personal actions: man's situation results from his having broken the Covenant with God."*

3. *"The situation first affects the human community as a whole by virtue of the fact of spiritual solidarity; every person is involved in it, from the moment of his entry through birth into that community."*

The three following theses express the spiritual *negativeness* of this state, which justifies the use of the term original *sin*, even where no positive resistance to God takes place. On this point, too, the doctrine of the Council of Trent and that of the Reformers readily agree:

4. *"This situation is not merely an absence of 'righteousness' or of a right relationship with God: even if it is not of the order of personal sin, it is still a state of rebellion."*

5. *"For humanity, one in Adam, is in opposition to its original vocation, which is to be a brotherly community in fellowship with God. This vocation, although rejected by man, is still upheld by God."*

6. *"Outside Christ, every human person is in a state of spiritual death, deprived of 'eternal life'."*

It was on the three following theses that agreement was, *a priori,* most unlikely, in view of the traditional Protestant affirmation and the traditional Catholic denial of the "total depravity of human nature". The theses state the area of agreement, but do not specify the residual disagreement revealed by the discussion, a disagreement bearing on a point of capital importance: the possibility of attaining a real knowledge of God by purely rational ways, a possibility which the Catholics hold and the Protestants reject.

The balanced character of these three theses is striking. Each one affirms both the impotence and the ability of fallen man, which limit each other. The controversy about the "enslaved will" seems here to have been by-passed, thanks to a clear and sober explanation of the Protestant statement, in Thesis 9.

7. *"Although we are dead to 'eternal life', there persists in us a vague aspiration towards God, incapable in itself of leading to a saving knowledge. No pursuit of human values, even ethical, belongs in its own right to the order of salvation: it remains ambiguous."*

8. *"As soon as it claims to be self-sufficient, this pursuit becomes sin; salvation cannot become effective unless human sufficiency dies. But the Holy Spirit can always arouse in us, through the appeal of various values, an authentic desire to seek God, and direct our steps towards the eschatological Kingdom."*

9. *"Incapable as we are of emerging from our state of sin through our own efforts, we none the less retain the responsibility for our actions and a certain ability to make decisions on the ethical level in our own strength."*

The most illuminating part of the discussion on original sin was on what was to form the substance of Theses 7 to 9, so that these were able to be accepted, not as equivocal compromises, but as real bases of agreement. The gist of this agreement can be expressed in these terms: There is not enough good remaining in fallen man for him to be self-sufficient without sin; but there remains enough good for justification not to suppress this by changing him into another person; justification saves him, liberates him, fulfils his personality by summoning him to a real personal submission to God. Which leads to the conclusion:

10. *"Under the action of the Holy Spirit and in dependence on Him, man makes his own response to the initiative of God who justifies him in Jesus Christ, and so performs the works of God 'who worketh in us both to will and to do'."*

Let us now examine more closely the joint theses which have been propounded since 1957 and which all deal with THE CHURCH.

In 1957 we desired to get to the heart of the Church's mission, beginning our study of this with *the mediation of Christ* and putting the emphasis on this mediation as it appears in the New Testament and on its relation to the Church's ministry. We deliberately held over to the following year the consideration of the mystery of the Church as the Body of Christ, a more difficult subject to approach and more likely to lead to disputes over its real meaning, so that we could limit our study to the essential functions of the Church and their significance. It was this which inspired the conclusion of these theses:

"These theses affirm the fact that the mediation of Christ reaches men in the Church and through her ministries. They do not define exactly the nature and the manner of their institution. They leave quite open the question of the mystery of the Church as the Body of Christ, but what still remains to be said of the Church as the Body of Christ cannot invalidate what has been said of the ministries of the Church."

Theses 1 and 2 set out the relationship between the mediation of Christ and the ministries of the Church:

1. *"There is one mediator between God and men, the man Christ Jesus."* 1 Tim. 2: 5.

2. *"The ministry of the Church is to bring all men into contact with this unique mediation. The mediation of Christ and the ministry of the Church are the two inseparable aspects of the action through which God reaches us in Jesus Christ. We can rightly speak of the Church's mediation in so far as we thereby express her instrumental function."*

Let us pause for a moment at the last sentence in Thesis 2: *"We can rightly speak of the Church's mediation in so far as we thereby express her instrumental function"* (relative to Christ, the sole mediator). At the 1957 gathering, the Catholics referred often to the mediation of the Church in this instrumental sense, and their Protestant colleagues admitted that the instrumental function of the Church could be expressed by the term mediation. Nevertheless, such a use of this term creates difficulties for most Protestants, as it seems to suggest a mediatorial function *superadded* to that of Christ in contradiction to His uniqueness. For that reason the Catholic members resorted to the word MINISTRY, since, from the standpoint of classical theology, the frequent use of the term MEDIATION was unnecessary. But all the theses explain in what sense the ministry of the Church is the special, but not unique, instrument through which Christ exercises His mediation in the course of history.

Theses 3–6 express in concrete terms this doctrine of the ministry of mediation by defining the relationship between the Word and the sacramental ministry and between these and the mediation of Christ.

It must be clearly expressed that salvation is *not only* an act of mediation performed *long ago* by the dying and risen Christ; this action intervenes in a specific and efficacious way, all through history, by means of the symbols through which Christ confronts men in the ministry of the Church. These symbols are at the same time *means of present efficacy* and *reminders of the historic event*, accomplished "once for all".

3. "*This instrumental function comprises in the Church the two-fold ministry of the Word and the Sacraments. In actual fact the mediation of Christ does not reach us simply by reminding us of an event in past history, however necessary this may be; it becomes operative in the present in the symbols of the Word and the Sacraments.*"

4. "*The Word is of the same order as the Sacrament in that it confronts men with the reality which is contemporary with us in the finished act of mediation. The Sacrament is of the same order as the Word in that a deliberate connection with the historical event on which this mediation is based is essential to its celebration.*"

5. "*When it relates the life of men to the historical event of Jesus Christ, and the Church herself to this centre of her life, the ministry of the Word is revealed as existing for the sole purpose of serving the mediatorial work of Jesus Christ. It precludes the Church from referring to herself except in so far as such references point to the source of her life: Christ crucified and risen.*"

6. "*Through the Sacrament, Christ Himself makes His mediation effectual in the Church, which rules out Donatism and magic. The sacraments are efficacious, not through the holiness of the ministry, nor yet by the material significance of the rite, but through the fact that they were instituted by Jesus Christ. Celebrated in accordance with His intention, they are endowed by Him, in the Holy Spirit, with the promised efficacy. For this reason, the Word which points to the intention of the Mediator is fundamental to the constitution of the Sacrament in the Church.*"

The last four theses indicate the dimensions of the Church's ministry: through the Church, Christ exercises His ministry of mediation throughout history; He sends the Church to all men, in every place. Because of this, all the members of the Church are in principle witnesses and agents of salvation, charged with the task of drawing all men to worship in spirit and in truth, invested with a "royal priesthood". Nevertheless the visible Church must avoid setting herself up as absolute and regarding her own life as the purpose of her mission (which is, in greater or less degree, the constant temptation which she faces): the true aim, the real meaning of her existence is the eschatological Kingdom, of which the pledges are given here and now in the Church terrestrial.

7. *"The priority of Christ's mediation, which is visible in an especial way in the ministry of the Word and Sacraments, must also mark the whole of the Church's life. The Church, in this passing age, guarantees the memory and the celebration (anamnesis) of the saving event of Christ which never passes away."*

8. *"By linking the Church to Jesus Christ, the ministry of the Word and Sacraments sets her in the service of men to reveal salvation to them. The ministry of the Word and Sacraments and the entire social structure of the Church are directed to the fulfilment of this mission. This ministry is not, however, the only means by which the mediation of Christ can reach men."*

9. *"Without prejudging the question of the sacerdotal ministry, which is open to debate among us, this universal mission which the Church derives from the mediation of Christ on behalf of the world implies a priesthood of believers."*

10. *"The goal of the Church is the Kingdom, the pledges of which are given to her, as a kind of first-fruits of the completed act of mediation. For this reason the Church stands in relation to the Kingdom as something more than a transitory instrument."*

In the discussion, the Protestants emphasized the Catholic tendency to set the Church up as an absolute society obsessed with her own activities. The idea of POWER, linked with that of office, is also wide open to dispute and misunderstanding, especially when applied exclusively to a clerical order. This will have to be studied later in an effort to see if power and office really contradict each other by suggesting appropriation of the "divine" by man on the one hand and man's service of God on the other.

We concluded the 1957 Theses by saying, among other things: *"These theses . . . leave quite open the question of the Church as the Body of Christ, but what still remains to be said of the Church as the Body of Christ cannot invalidate what has been said of her ministries."* There can be no question either of speaking of the Church, the Body of Christ, in such a way as to lead to the substitution of the Church for Christ, or of refusing to face the fact that, for Christ, the Church is His Body. It was this latter point that we studied at Presinge in 1958.[1]

Once more we were able to achieve a positive result by following our usual method: that of approaching each contentious subject from scriptural data. While openly admitting the very difficult emphases of the Catholic doctrine, which lays great stress on the organic nature of

[1] I am grateful to the Reverend Father Martelet, S.J., for the following notes on the 1958 Thesis; I was unable to be at the gathering that year. J. de B.

the Christ-Church relationship, and of Protestant doctrine which is apprehensive of the possible confusion of Christ and the Church:

1. *"We acknowledge that the New Testament witness to the mystery of the Body of Christ impels us not to sever ecclesiology from Christology, nor from pneumatology."*

Thesis 2 is an attempt to define the content of this scriptural affirmation. None of us regard the scriptural use of the expression "Body of Christ" as a mere metaphor. The affirmation presupposes a living relationship between Christ and the Church, which has her origin in Christ. The Protestants could not bring themselves to accept a conception, which they regard as too vitalistic, of the extension of the Incarnation; the Catholics, for their part, would never dream of giving it up. But to describe more precisely this living relationship of Christ to the Church, all that needs to be said at this point is that it results from the redemptive act of Christ and of His continued action in the Spirit.

2. *"In effect, when we say with Holy Scripture that the Church is the Body of Christ, this affirmation must not be taken as a mere metaphor: it expresses the mystery of the living relationship of Christ to His Church. He it is who, by His redemptive work, has founded her; He it is who, in the Spirit, gives her life, rules and guides her."*

When we think of the Church as thus established by Christ, we must say that she possesses, according to the testimony of the Scripture, a true organic life (especially Eph. 4). If we cannot agree among ourselves upon the precise definition of this organic life (cf. Thesis 8 of 1957) we can at least affirm that it results both from the will of Christ and from His present activity:

3. *"In so far as it appears visibly on earth, this Body has been ordained by the Lord who confers upon it a diversity of ministries and gifts."*

The anxiety of the Protestants on this point is lest Christ should be so completely identified with the Church that the distinction between the two should be compromised; the concern of the Catholics is that the life-giving union of Christ with the Church should as far as possible not be minimized. In fact it is in His capacity as Head, that is as Lord, that Christ unites the Church to Himself as Bride. This produced the following statement:

4. *"Jesus Christ is the Head of this Body, so that the organic unity which He has with His Church does not affect His lordship over her. This lordship establishes a distinction which does not compromise the reality of the relationship of Bridegroom and Bride which exists between Christ and His Church."*

It was difficult to reach agreement on how we could precisely express the exercise of Christ's lordship within the Church and at the same time His organic union with the Church. We were at least able to affirm that in this matter the Eucharist plays a decisive role; this was expressed in these terms:

5. *"Christ effects this union sacramentally by the gift of His body in the Eucharist."*

Once this claim had been established, the results of it were immediately apparent. In the light of the Eucharist, indeed, the life of the Church is seen as a life of holiness which is required and, in some ways, already realized. The Eucharist is truly a means of sanctification, since whoever receives it is embodied in Christ and identified with Him in the Spirit. The Eucharist also unites the members of the Body together and confers upon them the grace of drawing life from Christ as they live for their brethren. The fellowship thus realized is the level on which all differentiation of ministries must be thought out. Then followed the statement:

6. *"In this unity Christ calls His Church to holiness. He confers this gift upon the Church by granting to each member to be incorporated in Him and identified with Him in the Spirit. This incorporation in Christ makes us members one of another and enables us to experience our proper relationship to Christ in our relationship with our brethren.*

"The ministries have a special place in this twofold relationship."

In this list of common "theological grounds", supplied by Scripture, on the mystery of the Church as the Body of Christ, one last thing may be noted. Since the idea of a body necessarily implies unity in diversity and diversity in unity, Church order is not a non-essential addition but forms part of its very essence. This leads on to the last thesis:

7. *"Order in the Church is an essential manifestation of the life of the Body of Christ in its diversity and in its unity. Order is given to her as part of her very nature."*

Evidently, this still left undefined the exact nature of this order, admitted in general terms, and whether or not it implies the idea of hierarchical differentiation. The best approach to this problem seemed to be to face the question of authority, in a Church thus understood as the Body of Christ: *"Our research must be followed up by the study of the meaning of the Church's authority and of the relation of this authority to the Foundation."*

In 1959, therefore, we took up the question of pastoral *authority*. This was examined under several headings, but especially under that of the government of the community. On this point Catholicism clearly goes further than Calvin, and Calvin further than Luther and modern Protestants: in our conversations we have often been aware of this gulf between the confessional positions, despite a wide measure of agreement on scriptural data.

The 1959 Theses took for their foundation the agreement reached in 1957 on the Church's ministry, and still more on that reached in 1958 on the Church as the Body of Christ.

The first three underline the essential dependence and instrumentality which should mark pastoral authority in respect to Christ, the sole Lord and Shepherd:

1. *"Christ is the sole Lord, Head and Judge of the Church. In consequence, no authority can exist in the Church except that which is founded on Him and constantly submitted to His judgment."*

2. *"Christ, the chief Shepherd of His Church, exercises His authority in particular through ministers commissioned and aided by Him. These ministers are consecrated by the Church."*

3. *"The pastoral ministry, which includes the ministry of the Word and Sacraments, derives its authority from the fact that this ministry is the service of Christ exercised in the Church in the power of the Spirit."*

It is important to note that the agreement shown above has the effect of lessening the Protestant suspicion of an ecclesiastical authority rivalling that of Christ in the Catholic structure, and the Catholic suspicion of a desire for independence of effective "Christocracy" in the Protestant mistrust of priesthood and of all authority transmitted by "succession" in the Sacrament of Ordination.

Thesis 4 drew from the foregoing three conclusions which have a very important bearing on the relation of the authority of the ministers to the community of believers. We call particular attention to the third, which precludes at the same time the "democratic" interpretation in the Presbyterian-synodal system and the "aristocratic" interpretation in the Catholic system of authority transmitted by ordination:

"There follows from this:

(a) *That the authority of the ministry forms an integral part of the very nature of the Church;*

(b) *That it is ordained for the growth of the Body of Christ in holiness and truth, for the glory of God;*

43

(c) *That, without being delegated by the community, it is closely related to the building up of the community in charity and unity."*

The following three theses deduce from the first three further consequences which affect the person-to-person relationships between the minister invested with authority and the faithful who are under his charge:

The minister is a member of the fellowship;

Through the minister the obedience of the faithful is directed to Christ;

The minister must never lose sight, in practice, of the active presence of the Holy Spirit in his flock:

5. *"The relationship lies at the very heart of the fraternal relationship among the baptized, and at the same time transcends them."*

6. *"Obedience to the ministers must be offered as obedience to Jesus Christ the Lord; this safeguards Christian liberty."*

7. *"Respect for the personality of the baptized entails for the one who exercises authority the need on their behalf to be submissive to the Holy Spirit."*

Thesis 8 calls attention to the historical nature of the function of "authority" in the Church and at the same time the necessity of keeping in view that which lies beyond the Church's ministry, the final goal to which the whole gaze and the whole effort of the Christian people must be directed, the eschatological Kingdom:

8. *"Authority in the Church has for its goal: not only to assemble and to organize the community, to direct it towards its missionary tasks, but also to prepare it for the time when the ministries will come to an end and the community will be filled with the fulness of God."*

While agreement was reached on these theses as a whole, due attention was paid to the excessive and quite "unauthentic" nature of the authoritarianism often decried in Catholicism, and the democratic, if not anarchistic, tendency in ecclesiology which is sometimes observed in certain Protestant circles. What is authentic and fundamental on both sides is the "Christocracy" under which the Church claims to live. But there is a striking difference in the forms and methods which Catholics and Protestants attribute to this "Christocracy". One of the outstanding points of divergence is that of the transmission of authority, especially the Catholic doctrine of apostolic succession, the study of which was postponed to the following year.

Other questions which had been raised in the course of discussion were similarly left in abeyance. At the conclusion of the theses they were reduced to these four:

"*The exact relationship between ministerial authority and Scripture and the power of ordination;*

"*The different forms of the ministry and their relation to the Church;*

"*The necessity of a ministry which represents the universality of the Church;*

"*The existence of a magisterium and its relation to pastoral authority.*"

In 1960 "with fear and trembling" we faced the question of apostolic succession, which was the main cause of the disagreements between the Catholic and the Protestant members of our group.

So that we should not waste time following false trails, the Catholic position was stated as clearly as possible, with special reference to the joint Theses numbers 2, 5 and 7 of 1957 and numbers 1, 4 and 6 of 1959. When we speak of apostolic succession we are thinking chiefly of the episcopacy, but we must guard against dissociating the "powers" of the bishops from the *service* of the Church, which is their *raison-d'être*, and against losing sight of the pre-eminently *collegiate* nature of apostolic succession in the episcopacy. Unity is *conferred* by Christ on the episcopal body and on the whole Church, chiefly in fellowship with His Holy Spirit, but also in the ministerial function of the Pope.

The Pope is a valid symbol of unity in space, whereas episcopal ordination is a valid symbol of unity in time, the validity of the symbol being in both cases the work of the Holy Spirit. The Lord Jesus is the source of the succession, by the plenary powers given to the Apostles, as He is the source of the work of the Holy Spirit by His gift of the Spirit. "Why an uninterrupted succession going back to the Apostles? Because the historical continuity of the pastoral *college*, which is a fact, signifies identity of mission, and consequently links the obedience which we offer at this present time to Him who 'sent' the Apostles and 'sends' now their successors to guard loyally and to communicate to all men the 'deposit' laid down by them in Scripture and in the community which draws its life from it (cf. Matt. 28: 20)." (Introductory Catholic Statement.)

In the same introductory statement the "Sacramental nature" of ordination is explained in these terms: "Christ, when he makes a man His 'envoy', takes possession of him and *consecrates* him in his very personality: what is valid for the Christian 'set apart' *in* the world as witness for Jesus Christ is equally valid for the bishop 'set apart' *in* the Church as representative of the one Shepherd, as an instrument of Christ the Head."

Whereas the Catholics stress the continuity which links the apostles to the bishops, the Protestants emphasize what was unique and intransmissible in the apostolic function, while fully admitting that the Apostles invested the first bishops and presbyters in the name of Christ, and, in this sense, transmitted to them a pastoral authority. They insist emphatically that the authority thus transmitted always has as its basis and norm the apostolic teaching laid down in the New Testament writings and possesses no infallibity except that of these writings.

The Catholic position is more concerned about the authenticity of the *mission of the spokesmen* of Christ, the Protestant position about the authenticity of the apostolic *message* delivered by these men.

The Protestants would readily admit, in a sense which is limited by the above comments, an "apostolic succession" in the ministry of *the whole Church*, whereas the Catholics call that the apostolicity of the Church and attribute to the bishops, and to themselves, an apostolic succession in a clearly *pastoral* sense.

Distinct differences of emphasis and even significant divergences still persist. Despite that, we were able to reach agreement on six theses which are of considerable interest.

The first links the apostolicity of the Church with its Christological origins and, in particular, with the 1958 Theses on the Church as the Body of Christ:

1. *"The Church is apostolic in its very essence, because it is the Body of Him who, sent by the Father, in His turn sent the Church into the world."*

Four theses follow which mark out the area of agreement. There is room for a distinction in the mission of the Apostles between an intransmissible element (their role as a "constituent" assembly in the matter of the witness and the structure of the Church) and a transmissible element (their missionary and pastoral responsibility):

2. *"This apostolicity is founded on Christ's commission to the Apostles, which comprises a transmissible element and an intransmissible element."*

3. *"The intransmissible element: the Apostles were chosen to be the authorized eye-witnesses of the redemptive event and to form the foundation on which the Lord builds His Church. Their testimony is deposited in the writings of the New Testament."*

4. *"The transmissible element: the command to proclaim the Gospel and to build up the Church. Since the apostolic age, the fulfilment of this command is still being continued in the Church on the foundation laid by the Apostles and must remain wholly faithful to the 'deposit' handed on by them. There is, then, an apostolic succession."*

The ministry of the Apostles' successors must be constantly submitted to the witness and the doctrine of the Apostles. That does not mean, however, that the dependence of the Church on the *reading* of the New Testament writings is in one direction only; we need the Church so that we may understand the Gospel message and live a healthy Christian life:

5. "*The content of the apostolic 'deposit' cannot be determined without reference, at least implicitly, to the Scripture as the norm. But Scripture sends us back to the Church to whom it is entrusted. The 'deposit' can only be fully understood as it is experienced in the Church, under the guidance of the Holy Spirit.*"

Thesis 6, by way of conclusion, brings us right back to the christological perspective by emphasizing that the influence of Christ on the "apostolic succession" is not confined to the fact that He commissioned the Apostles *of old*: all through Christian history, the Lord intervenes as the source and at the same time as the goal of the ministry.

6. "*The charge transmitted by the Apostles is constantly accepted in the Church by the ministers whom the Lord gives to His body. This transmission is in the service of Christ alone and offered to the world.*"

This agreement, interesting as it is, covers only a part of the subject matter which we discussed in 1960. We raised, as a postscript, four questions which had still to be discussed:

"*The relation between the ministries and apostolic succession.*"

In other words, is this succession inherent in every ministry of the Church or only in that of bishops (through the instrumentality of which, at the very least, other ministries have their ground and inspiration)?

"*The collegiate aspect of these ministries*" (exercised by the successors of the Apostles).

"*Their sacerdotal character.*"

"*Their (charismatic) gift of infallibility.*"

It was the third of these questions which was eventually chosen as the subject for the 1961 gathering, under the heading: PRIESTHOOD AND MINISTRY IN THE CHURCH.

That was an especially delicate subject! Between the 1960 and 1961 gatherings, the Lyons team were to devote two or three sessions to preparing for it and the same number of sessions during the following scholastic year; we shall see the reason for this.

Despite the earlier agreement and the direct preparation, the 1961 gathering did not end with any joint theses, but in stalemate. Why?

To some extent because the subject was a difficult one, but also the group which usually met was somewhat thrown out of balance by the absence of a few experienced members and by an unusual influx of new members, and because the method which had been used over the preceding years was not regularly followed.

This is the essence of the conclusions reached in common in 1961:

"*We encountered a difficulty: the role of the minister in the communication of these fruits*" (*the fruits of the unique priestly mediation of Jesus Christ*); "*a difficulty which was particularly evident in the matter of the eucharistic celebration. For some, indeed, this celebration does not imply a priesthood other than that of the whole Church, vested in each of her members. For others, it demands a special ministry which is specifically sacerdotal. The difficulty which Protestants encounter in the Catholic position arises mainly from the fact that this sacerdotal ministry appears to obscure or to duplicate both the mediation of Christ and the priesthood of believers. The difficulty which Catholics find in the Protestant position lies in the fact that the true nature of the sacerdotal role of the unique Mediator is not made clearly manifest to His Body.*

"*Assuredly, we all admit that the Church, the Body of Christ, is a sacerdotal body in the sense of 1 Peter 2: 5 ff. For this reason, whatever may be the answer that we have to give to the question raised by the ministerial priesthood, this can only be thought of as a function of the spiritual priesthood of believers and as a function of the Christ-Church relationship. The task which faces us is to discover what is the testimony of the Scripture on the priesthood of the New Covenant and on the question of a ministerial priesthood.*"

In 1962, we had to return to the previous year's subject, seeking new ways of approach to it and applying to it the methods which had proved successful in our discussions.

Even more definitely than on previous occasions, Christology was our point of departure: how is Christ's sacrifice to be understood? Can it become efficacious for us today in a sacramental way through the ministry of the Church and, above all, in the eucharistic celebration? This question determined the theme of the gathering: THE SACERDOTAL ACTION OF CHRIST IN THE SACERDOTAL ACTIVITY OF THE CHURCH.

This concern was clearly apparent in the Prologue to the agreed theses: "*We have studied the relationship between the personal nature of Christ and the sacramental nature of His gifts in order to try to discover whether or not the transmission of these gifts through the Church implied a ministry endowed with a special sacerdotal character.*"

The first two theses record our agreement on the most general Christological foundations; the mediation of Christ presupposes a sustained and intimate union with men who are being saved, particularly in and through the Church which is His Body. If the sacrifice of Christ saves us, it cannot be simply by the substitution of Christ for ourselves, but even more by the *"recapitulation"* of ourselves in Him, the "new Adam", the New Man whom we "put on" at Baptism. This "recapitulation" would be entirely fictitious if there were not *now* (at the present moment in our lives) a *presence* of Christ active in us and for us, a presence of the Risen Christ in His twofold action as priest and victim of the redemptive sacrifice (unique, unrepeatable, accomplished long ago on the Cross).

1. *"The unique character of the mediation of Christ, incarnate Son of God, king and priest after the order of Melchizedek, does not imply His separation from men, but, on the contrary, their recapitulation in Him who is Lord of the world and Head of His Church."*

2. *"Christ is present now in His Church as the living Lord who has ascended into glory. He who was crucified is also He who is risen. It is by participating in His living presence that we share, through the Holy spirit, in the Action by which He saves us."*

His redemptive action is based on the "communicability" of the *being* of Christ. This being and this action are both absolutely *unique*, but of a *uniqueness* so full and comprehensive that, far from excluding our participation in them, it justifies and calls forth our participation. For it was for us and for our salvation that the Son of God became incarnate, and in view of what salvation is, we cannot profit by the fruits of His redemptive action without, in some way, participating personally *in this action itself*, through the mediation of the Word and Sacraments.

If, as the Catholics believe, there is a special priesthood for the Ministry of the Word and Sacraments, conferred by a special sacrament, this priesthood is none other than the efficacious sign through which Christ the Head exerts His decisive influence and demonstrates His absolute lordship over the Church which is His Body, by associating her with His sacrifice in a situation of real dependence and receptivity.

3. *"The redemptive Act of Christ on the cross, accomplished once for all, cannot be repeated; but its power is eternally active in the perpetual intercession of the Son, the eternal High-Priest, with the Father."*

4. *"Accomplished by the Son, as Head of the Body, the redemptive act*

in Jesus Christ is available for us all and comes to full fruition only in us. Its nature is such that it must be shared."

5. *"Through faith, the Church shares in the act of Her redemption; she is thus conformed in her members to the Mystery of her Head."*

6. *"The Body is thus conformed to its Head only by the initiative of the Head and in His power. The exercise of initiative must be made apparent in the very centre of the Church."*

The following thesis is no more than a *résumé* of the 1957 Theses. This reminder was necessary to remove the embarrassment caused on both sides by confessional habits of thinking: a stronger emphasis on the Word by the Protestants, on the Sacrament by the Catholics. Our ideas had to be clarified on the way the Risen Christ is present in His sacrifice on the Cross and enables us to share in it:

7. *"The power of Christ the Head is fully exerted only in the conjunction of the Word and the Sacrament, which complement each other. The Word leads to the Sacrament. The Sacrament makes the content of the Word come alive in a new way; the Word gives meaning to the Sacrament and guards it from error (preventing it from degenerating into magic or superstition, etc.)."*

The discussion brought out the different sense in which Catholics and Protestants used terms which refer to the sacrificial rite, especially in their (analogous) application to the death of Christ. SACRIFICE, IMMOLATION, EXPIATION, OFFERING are perennial sources of misunderstanding, partly on account of what each reads into these terms, but even more on account of what each one thinks is implied when someone on the other side uses them. It is futile to explain our mutual positions, we still remain conditioned by a past full of controversies in which divergences have been exaggerated beyond all reason. The traditional terminology of sacrifice had to be dispensed with if we were to understand exactly what each meant.

Moreover, the images in which thought is clothed cause fresh difficulties. Especially is it easy to set the idea of the Eucharist as the gift of God to man (downward movement) over against the idea of the Eucharist as an offering by man to God (upward movement), particularly when one has come under the influence of A. Nygren (*Eros et Agapé*) and of G. Aulen (*Christus Victor*). This explains the tendency on the part of some Protestants to find some incompatibility between the idea of the Eucharist as a sacramental gift of God in Jesus Christ and the idea of the Eucharist as an offering of Christ made by the Church to the Father.

But no real difficulty is experienced in the thought that the same act of Christ may be, in itself and in its sacramental actualization, at one and the same time the gift of the Son from the Father to man and homage offered by the total Christ (comprising Divine-human Head and the Church His Body). In fact, Christ on the cross loves both His Father and men to the point of accepting death by obedience to God for the salvation of men; and today He cannot truly give Himself to us without linking us with the filial homage towards the Father which inspires His whole existence at the deepest level, and so without, in some way, actively associating us with the offering of Himself and the Church His Body in the *memorial* of the cross. For a memorial, in the Biblical sense, cannot exist unless the fundamental intentions of the original act are there encountered.

Thesis 8 expresses the *partial* agreement reached, on the subject of the "sacramental sacrifice" of the Eucharist, by avoiding the familiar technical terms which give rise to ambiguities and by stressing these basic truths:

8. *"By giving Himself in the Eucharist to the Church, Christ draws her with Him in His own movement towards the Father, a movement of consecration, of life in death. Thus He gives her a part in His own offering of praise to the Father and in His power to intercede for the salvation of the world. In that way the Church, the Body of Christ the High Priest, is revealed as being a sacerdotal people."*

The qualities of ministerial priesthood is therefore not dealt with directly in the theses which emerged from the 1962 assembly, although it had been discussed at length in the preceding conversations. But we were able to reach an agreement on its deepest presuppositions, and henceforth we have a better chance of making progress in the study of this question by relying on the overall agreement reached from 1957 to 1962. The latest expression of agreement was:

"We have not exhausted the meaning of the Eucharist. It seems possible from now on to raise the problem of the ministry, as the service of Christ in its relation to His Body."

J. DE BACIOCCHI, S.M., Lyon.

IV

THE THESES
FOLLOWED BY A BIBLIOGRAPHY

THE STATE OF ORIGINAL SIN (1956)

The group of Catholic theologians and Protestant pastors which has been meeting for many years, sometimes at Les Dombes, sometimes at Presinge or Taizé, has devoted its meetings this summer to the doctrinal study: "Man as a sinner, the Christian man". Having reached an agreement, the group thought it necessary to draw up the following theses so as to set out in a precise manner the results of its ecumenical research.

They feel that other groups, engaged in the same research, may, without attributing to these theses an authority which their authors do not possess in their respective Churches, be encouraged in their ecumenical work by the reading of this publication and may give attention to the way this group has gone about its task.

The agreement which the group has reached rests upon two fundamental declarations.

The conflicts in the sixteenth century sprang to a large degree from different concerns. Whereas in the expression "human nature" the Catholic Church had in mind the ontological status of man, the Reformers, inspired by their essentially soteriological concern, took it to include the relationship of man with God.

Moreover, we have been able to look at the whole question afresh, because we have studied it as a dilemma of nature and as a dilemma of personality, and have thus been able to reach a view of original sin which takes human solidarity into account.

It must, however, be pointed out that, in these theses, we have not dealt with the question whether or not one can know God through human reason.

1. Our redemption in Jesus Christ makes clear to us that outside that redemption we are subject to the rule of sin.

2. The state of sin lies at the root of all our personal actions; man's situation results from his having broken the Covenant with God.

3. This situation first affects the human community as a whole; by virtue of the fact of human solidarity, every person is involved in it, from the moment of his entry through birth into that community.

4. This situation is not merely an absence of "righteousness" or of a right relationship with God; even if it is not of the order of personal sin, it is still a state of rebellion.

5. For humanity, one in Adam, is in opposition to its original vocation, which is to be a brotherly community in fellowship with God. This vocation, although rejected by man, is still upheld by God.

6. Outside Christ, every human person is in a state of spiritual death, deprived of "eternal life".

7. Although we are dead to "eternal life", there persists in us a vague aspiration towards God, incapable in itself of leading to a saving knowledge. No pursuit of human values, even ethical, belongs in its own right to the order of salvation: it remains ambiguous.

8. As soon as it claims to be self-sufficient, this pursuit becomes sin; salvation cannot become effective unless human sufficiency dies. But the Holy Spirit can always arouse in us, through the appeal of various values, an authentic desire to seek God and direct our steps towards the eschatological Kingdom.

9. Incapable as we are of emerging from our state of sin through our own efforts, we none the less retain the responsibility for our actions and a certain ability to make decisions on the ethical level in our own strength.

10. Under the action of the Holy Spirit and in dependence on Him, man makes his own response to the initiative of God who justifies him in Jesus Christ, and so performs the works of God "who worketh in us both to will and to do."

THE MEDIATION OF CHRIST AND THE MINISTRY OF THE CHURCH
(1957)

1. There is one mediator between God and men, the man Jesus Christ (1 Tim. 2: 5).

2. The ministry of the Church is to bring all men into contact with this unique mediation. The mediation of Christ and the ministry of the Church are two inseparable aspects of the action through which God reaches us in Jesus Christ. We can rightly speak of the Church's mediation in so far as thereby we express her instrumental function.

3. This instrumental function comprises in the Church the two-fold ministry of the Word and the Sacraments. In actual fact the media-

tion of Christ does not reach us simply by reminding us of an event in past history, however necessary this may be; it becomes operative in the present in the symbols of the Word and the Sacraments.

4. The Word is of the same order as the Sacrament in that it confronts men with the reality which is contemporary with us in the finished act of mediation. The Sacrament is of the same order as the Word in that a deliberate connection with the historical event on which this mediation is based is essential to its celebration.

5. When it relates the life of men to the historical event of Jesus Christ, and the Church herself to this centre of her life, the Ministry of the Word is revealed as existing for the sole purpose of serving the mediatorial work of Christ. It precludes the Church from referring to herself except in so far as such references point to the source of her life: Christ crucified and risen.

6. Through the Sacrament, Christ Himself makes His mediation effectual, which rules out Donatism and magic. The sacraments are efficacious, not through the holiness of the minister, nor yet by the material significance of the rite, but through the fact that they were instituted by Jesus Christ. Celebrated in accordance with His intention, they are endowed by Him, in the Holy Spirit, with the promised efficacy. For this reason, the Word which points to the intention of the Mediator is fundamental to the constitution of the Sacrament in the Church.

7. The priority of Christ's mediation, which is visible in an especial way in the ministry of the Word and Sacraments, must also mark the whole of the Church's life. The Church, in this passing age, guarantees the memory and the celebration (anamnesis) of the saving event of Christ which never passes away.

8. By linking the Church to Jesus Christ, the ministry of the Word and Sacraments sets her in the service of men to reveal salvation to them. The ministry of the Word and Sacraments and the entire social structure of the Church are directed to the fulfilment of this mission. This ministry is not, however, the only means by which the mediation of Christ can reach men.

9. Without prejudging the question of the sacerdotal ministry, which is open to debate among us, this universal mission which the Church derives from the mediation of Christ on behalf of the world implies a priesthood of believers.

10. The goal of the Church is the Kingdom, the pledges of which are given to her, as a kind of first-fruits of the completed act of media-

tion. For this reason the Church stands in relation to the Kingdom as something more than a transitory instrument.

These theses affirm the fact that the mediation of Christ reaches men in the Church through her ministries. They do not define exactly the nature and the manner of their institution. They leave quite open the question of the mystery of the Church as the Body of Christ, but what still remains to be said of the Church as the Body of Christ cannot invalidate what has been said of her ministries.

THE CHURCH, THE BODY OF CHRIST (1958)

1. We acknowledge that the New Testament witness to the mystery of the Body of Christ impels us not to sever ecclesiology from Christology, nor from pneumatology.

2. In effect, when we say with the Holy Scripture that the Church is the Body of Christ, this affirmation must not be taken as a mere metaphor; it expresses the mystery of the living relationship of Christ to His Church. He it is who, by His redemptive work has founded her; He it is who, in the spirit, gives her life, rules and guides her.

3. In so far as it appears visibly on the earth, this Body has been ordained by the Lord who confers upon it a diversity of ministries and gifts.

4. Jesus Christ is the Head of this Body, so that the organic unity which He has with His Church does not affect His lordship over her. This lordship establishes a distinction which does not compromise the relationship of Bridegroom and Bride which exists between Christ and His Church.

5. Christ effects this union sacramentally by the gift of His body in the Eucharist.

6. In this unity Christ calls His Church to holiness. He confers this gift upon the Church by granting to each member to be incorporated in Him and identified with Him in the Spirit. This incorporation in Christ makes us members one of another and enables us to experience our proper relationship to Christ in our relationships with our brethren.

The ministries have a special place in this twofold relationship.

7. Order in the Church is an essential manifestation of the life of the Body of Christ in its diversity and in its unity. Order is conferred upon her as part of her very nature.

Our research must be followed up by the study of the meaning of the Church's authority and of the relation of this authority to its Foundation.

PASTORAL AUTHORITY IN THE CHURCH

Referring to the thesis of 1958 on the living relationship of Christ with the Church which is His Body, we reaffirm that Christ, through His redemptive work, founded the Church and that, in the Spirit, He gives her life, rules and directs her.

1. Christ is the sole Lord, Head and Judge of the Church. In consequence, no authority can exist in the Church except that which is founded on Him, and constantly submitted to His judgment.

2. Christ, the chief Shepherd of His Church, exercises His authority in particular through ministers commissioned and aided by Him. These ministers are consecrated by the Church.

3. The pastoral ministry, which includes the ministry of the Word and Sacraments, derives its authority from the fact that this ministry is the service of Christ exercised in the Church in the power of the Spirit.

4. There follows from this:
    (a) That the authority of the ministry forms an integral part of the very nature of the Church;
    (b) That it is ordained for the growth of the Body of Christ in holiness and truth, for the glory of God;
    (c) That, without being delegated by the community, it is closely related to the building up of the community in charity and unity.

5. The relationship of authority is at the very heart of the fraternal relationships among the baptized, and at the same time transcends them.

6. Obedience to the ministers must be offered as obedience to Jesus Christ the Lord; this safeguards Christian liberty.

7. Respect for the personality of the baptized entails for the one who exercises authority the need, on their behalf, to be submissive to the Holy Spirit.

8. Authority in the Church has for its goal, not only to assemble and to organize the community, to direct it towards its missionary tasks, but also to prepare it for the time when the ministries will come to an end and the community will be filled with the fulness of God.

These theses leave the following questions open:
   The nature of the apostolic College and of its succession;
   The exact relationship between ministerial authority and Scripture and the power of ordination;

The different forms of the ministry and their relation to the nature of the Church;

The necessity of a ministry which represents the universality of the Church;

The existence of a magisterium and its relation to pastoral authority.

THE APOSTOLICITY OF THE CHURCH (1960)

1. The Church is apostolic in its very essence, because it is the Body of Him who, sent by the Father, in His turn sent the Church into the world.

2. This apostolicity is founded on Christ's commission to the apostles, which comprises a transmissible element and an intransmissible element.

3. The intransmissible element: the Apostles were chosen to be the authorized eye-witnesses of the redemptive event and to form the foundation on which the Lord builds His Church. Their testimony is deposited in the writings of the New Testament.

4. The transmissible element: the command to proclaim the Gospel and to build up the Church. Since the apostolic age, the fulfilment of this command is still being continued in the Church on the foundation laid by the Apostles and must remain wholly faithful to the "deposit" handed on by them. There is, then, an apostolic succession.

5. The content of the apostolic "deposit" cannot be determined without reference, at least implicitly, to the Scripture as the norm. But Scripture sends us back to the Church to whom it is entrusted. The "deposit" can only be fully understood as it is experienced in the Church, under the guidance of the Holy Spirit.

6. The charge transmitted by the Apostles is constantly accepted in the Church by the ministers whom the Lord gives to His Body. This transmission is in the service of Christ alone and offered to the world.

These affirmations leave the following questions open:

The relation between the ministries and apostolic succession;

The collegiate aspect of these ministries;

Their sacerdotal character;

Their charismatic gift of infallibility.

These questions must be made clear and supplemented by the Theses of the years 1957-59 on: the ministry, the Church as the Body of Christ, and pastoral authority.

PRIESTHOOD AND MINISTRY OF THE CHURCH (1961)

The question with which we dealt in the course of the present session, "Priesthood and Ministry of the Church", was so difficult that we were unable to draw up any theses which expressed precise doctrinal agreement on this subject. At the same time, in view of subsequent proceedings, we felt it necessary to make the following declarations.

We declare our belief in the unique priesthood of Jesus Christ, in the terms already stated: "There is one mediator between God and men, the man Christ Jesus" (1 Tim. 2: 5). Further, we reaffirm that "The ministry of the Church is to bring all men into contact with this unique mediation. The mediation of Christ and the ministry of the Church are two inseparable aspects of the action through which God reaches us in Jesus Christ. We can rightly speak of the Church's mediation in so far as thereby we express her instrumental function" (1957, Theses 1, 2).

But it was clear to us, this year, that we could only grasp the full significance of these affirmations by defining the way in which the fruits of the priestly mediation of Christ are made available to us in His Church. Here we encountered a difficulty: the role of the minister in the communication of these fruits, a difficulty which was particularly evident in the matter of the eucharistic celebration.

For some, this celebration does not imply a priesthood other than that of the whole Church, vested in each of its members. For others, it demands a special ministry which is specifically sacerdotal.

The difficulty which Protestants encounter in the Catholic position arises mainly from the fact that this sacerdotal ministry appears to obscure or to duplicate both the mediation of Christ and the priesthood of believers. The difficulty which Catholics find in the Protestant position lies in the fact that the true nature of the sacerdotal role of the unique Mediator is not made clearly manifest to His Body.

Assuredly, we all admit that the Church, the Body of Christ, is a sacerdotal body in the sense of 1 Pet. 2: 5 ff. For this reason, whatever may be the answer that we have to give to the question raised by the ministerial priesthood, this can only be thought of as a function of the spiritual priesthood of believers and as a function of the Christ-Church relationship.

The task which faces us is to discover what is the testimony of the Scripture on the priesthood of the New Covenant and on the question of a ministerial priesthood.

THE SACERDOTAL ACTION OF CHRIST IN THE SACERDOTAL ACTIVITY OF THE CHURCH (1962)

We studied the relationship between the personal nature of Christ and the sacramental nature of His gifts in order to try to discover whether or not the transmission of these gifts through the Church implied a ministry endowed with a special sacerdotal character.

1. The unique character of the mediation of Christ, incarnate Son of God, King and Priest after the order of Melchizedek, does not imply His separation from men, but on the contrary their recapitulation in Him who is Lord of the World and Head of His Church.

2. Christ is present now in His Church as the Living Lord who has ascended into glory. He who was crucified is also He who is risen. It is by participating in His living presence that we are able to share, through the Holy Spirit, in the Action by which He saves us.

3. The redemptive Act of Christ on the cross, accomplished once for all, cannot be repeated; but its power is eternally active in the perpetual intercession of the Son, the eternal High Priest, with the Father.

4. Accomplished by the Son as Head of the body, the redemptive Act is available in Jesus Christ for us all and comes to full fruition only in us. Its nature is such that it must be shared.

5. Through faith the Church shares in the Act of her Redemption. She is thus conformed in her members to the Mystery of her Head.

6. The Body is thus conformed to its Head only by the initiative of the Head and in His power. The exercise of this initiative must be made apparent in the very centre of the Church.

7. The power of Christ the Head is fully exerted only in the conjunction of the Word and the Sacraments, which complement each other. The Word leads to the Sacrament. The Sacrament makes the content of the Word come alive in a new way; the Word gives meaning to the Sacrament and guards it from error.

8. By giving Himself in the Eucharist to the Church, Christ draws her with Him in His own movement towards the Father, a movement of consecration and renunciation, of life in death. He gives her a part in His own offering of praise to the Father and in His power to intercede for the salvation of the world. In that way the Church, the Body of Christ the High Priest, is revealed as being a sacerdotal people.

We have not exhausted the meaning of the Eucharist. It seems possible from now on to raise the question of the ministry, as the service of Christ in its relation to His Body.

BIBLIOGRAPHY

Meeting 1946 (Tradition)

M. Thurian, *Développement du dogme et tradition selon le Catholicisme moyen et la théologie réformée*, Verbum Caro, I (1947), pp. 145–67.

Meeting 1948 (Prophecy, Mariology)

M. Thurian, *Mariology*, in *Ways of Worship, the Report of a Theological Commission of Faith and Order*, London, (1951), pp. 289–323.

Meeting 1950 (The Sacraments)

J. de Baciocchi, *Les sacrements, actes libres du Seigneur*, Nouvelle Revue Théologique, LXXIII (1951), pp. 681–706.

Meeting 1951

P. Michalon, *L'Eglise, corps mystique du Christ glorieux*, Nouvelle Revue Théologique, LXXIV (1952), pp. 673–87.

Meeting 1953 (Meditation on the Lord's Prayer)

G. Martelet, *Remets-nous nos dettes*, Verbum Caro, X (1956), pp. 79–84.

Meeting 1954 (Christ)

J. de Senarclens, *La Christologie de Karl Barth*, Foi et Vie, LIII (1955), pp. 1–25.

Meeting 1955 (The Holy Spirit)

J. de Baciocchi, *Comment reconnaître la personnalité du Saint-Esprit?*, Nouvelle Revue Théologique, LXVII (1955), pp. 1025–49.

Meeting 1956 (Man as sinner)

J. de Baciocchi, *Vues catholiques sur l'état de péché originel*, Verbum Caro, XI (1957), pp. 88–103.

G. Martelet, *Le mystère de corps et de l'Esprit dans le Christ ressuscité et dans l'Eglise*, Verbum Caro, XII (1958), pp. 31–53.

Meeting 1958 (The Church as Body of Christ)

P. Bonnard, *L'Eglise corps du Christ dans le paulinisme*, Revue de théologie et de philosophie, VIII (1958), pp. 268–82.

Meeting 1959 (Pastoral authority in the Church)

J. Cadet, *L'autorité pastorale dans la pratique de l'Eglise catholique*, Verbum Caro, XIV (1960), pp. 115–35.

J.-J. von Allmen, *L'autorité pastorale d'après les confessions de foi réformées*, ibid., pp. 202–16.

Meeting 1960 (Apostolicity of the Church)

P. Bonnard, *Le N.T. connaît-il la transmission d'une fonction apostolique?* Verbum Caro, XV (1961), pp. 132–37.

J. Colson, *La succession apostolique au niveau du premier siècle*, ibid., pp. 138–72.

A. Benoit, *L'apostolicité au deuxième siècle, ibid.*, pp. 173–84.

G. Martelet, *Eléments transmissibles et intransmissibles de la succession apostolique, ibid.*, pp. 185–98.

Meeting 1961 (Priesthood and Ministry)

P.-A. Harlé, *Sacerdoce et ministère dans le N.T., Verbum Caro*, XV (1961), pp. 357–71.

J. Bosc, *Ministère et sacerdoce universel en doctrine réformée, ibid.*, pp. 372–77.

J. de Baciocchi, *Ministère et médiation sacerdotale, ibid.*, pp. 378–89.

V

CONCLUSION

A PROTESTANT POINT OF VIEW

AT THE OUTSET, it would be useful to pass some observations on the way these present theses were drawn up.

Father M. Villain, in an earlier chapter in this work and in his books, has given us a vivid description of the origin of these gatherings[1] and of the conversations that took place there.[2] I should like, at this point, to recall two aspects of these conversations which, in my opinion, have made possible the publication of these joint theses.

1. The intention which lay behind our theological research was the attempt to discover what was the *root* of our dogmatic differences. In the first place we had to inquire whether we had the same view of the Person of Christ. Our Churches claimed to hold in common the Chalcedonian formula; did we put the same interpretation on it? Now the 1954 gathering enabled us to give an affirmative answer to this question but also made us aware of a fundamental difference; whereas the Catholic theologians regard the Chalcedonian formula as a revealed statement, valid in itself, a conceptual statement of the truth about Christ, the Protestant theologians look upon this dogma as the outcome of a long history: rediscovering all its premises in apostolic thought, they affirm that, when in the course of the first centuries the Church formulated this dogma, she was utterly obedient to the Holy Scripture where she discovered, amid the manifold doctrines formulated at that time, the truth about Christ. The Church thus removed from her life errors which in the end would have been fatal to her unity and fidelity. As we studied the same dogma from very different angles, we were led to recognize that these views were *complementary*. Evidently it was a question of differing emphases rather than of radically distinctive

---

[1] *L'abbé Paul Couturier, ed. Casterman*, 1957, p. 161 ff.

[2] *Introduction à l'oecuménisme (Coll. Eglise Vivante)*, ed. Casterman, 1958, p. 212 ff.

views. Our consideration of each other's outlook and way of thinking gave to our faith in the Person of Christ, as the Fathers of the Council had described it, a new richness compounded of exactness and vitality. This discovery drove us to the point where we agreed that each one of us should express his faith in his own language, in his own intellectual and spiritual climate, without branding them in advance as different, in short to "recognize" each other for what we are. The joint theses drawn up between 1956 and 1962 bear the marks of this "recognition". Traditional Catholic language and traditional Protestant language sometimes are blended; at other times both are abandoned in favour of new formulations. This may prove an obstacle for readers who have not taken part in drawing up the theses. It is our hope that the Protestant reader, in particular, will try to find in this collection not what fits in with his denominational ideas, but what points to the complementary views assembled here, even if the questions on which agreement was not reached are put in a footnote at the end of the theses.

2. The 1956 Theses state how, in dealing with a subject as crucial as that of the state of sin, intimately linked with that of justification by faith, we were able to look at the theme as a whole. When the controversy over nature, which dominated the polemics of the sixteenth century, was interpreted in the light of the question of the individual, a whole series of misunderstandings was cleared up and we were able to make a new and illuminating statement. This had an influence on the theses as a whole; they were drawn up with an emphasis on a "universe of personal relations", in which man's situation with regard to God and God's situation with regard to man are the central considerations.

Thus one of the elements which dominated the theses on the Church was the notion of *instrumentality* (1957, Thesis 2); for this notion cannot be reduced to a static concept, it expresses the role and the functions of the Church, it defines the relations between Christ and the Church, between Christ and the ministers of the Church, between the members of the Church and humanity as a whole. It might even have been vitally important to apply this dynamic, personal and communal idea to the doctrine of the Trinity on a much wider basis, linked not only to the Church but to the creature and creation on one hand and to pneumatic eschatology on the other.

It seems to me that it is due to this relational point of view that our studies did not founder in arguments about the institution-event, as it helped us to speak of the Church in another way.

As we look back over the conversation out of which the theses arose, there are two impressions:

1. First, that we set the ecclesiological problems which divide us in the right perspective—*referring the Church to Christ*.

Certainly, in 1957, we made use of an abstract philosophical term: Christ, the Foundation of the Church (Thesis 5); taking our stand on the 1958 Thesis, we can interpret this in a more concrete sense, that of Head of the Church, or that of foundation as is intended in 1 Cor. 3: 11; but the thought was clear. It was because of this guiding line of thought that we were able successively to study the different aspects of the work of Christ and of the Person of Christ in order to clarify the nature of the Church and her ministries. *Because* Christ is the Mediator between God and men, and because the mission of the Church is to bring all men into touch with this mediation, we were able to affirm that "the mediation of Christ and the ministry of the Church are two inseparable aspects of the action through which God reaches us in Jesus Christ" (1957, Thesis 2).

Now that was the very foundation of all our thought about the relationship between what we understand of the work of Christ and what we affirm concerning the Church's task: the consequential, subordinate nature of the Church which is, at the same time, bound to Christ in an indissoluble union. We avoided, at one and the same time, any idea of *confusion* between the two or of *separation* and especially— and this is the most subtle temptation—of simple *co-existence* on two different planes, the celestial and the terrestrial. This is what we had to define more closely in 1958, in Thesis 4, in a statement which is basic to our common ecclesiology: "Jesus Christ is the Head of this Body, so that the organic unity which He has with His Church does not affect His lordship over her. This lordship establishes *a distinction which does not compromise the reality of the relationship* of Bridegroom and Bride which exists between Christ and His Church." We discover the same perspective when we examine the link between the sovereignty of Christ and the Ministries (1959, Theses 1 and 2), between Jesus Christ sent by God and the apostolicity of the Church (1960, Thesis 1). This same reason enabled us, when we thought about the sacerdotal act of Christ (1962), to make the joint affirmation: "*The unique character of the mediation of Christ . . . does not imply His separation from men, but on the contrary, their recapitulation in Him . . .*" (1962, Thesis 1). It was the thought of the mediation of the redemptive act of the crucified and risen Christ which led us to a solidarist view of human sin; it was the same truth which determined our thought on the recapitulation of all men in Christ.

"*Accomplished by the Son, as Head of the Body, the redemptive act in Jesus Christ is available for us all and comes to full fruition only in us. Its nature is such that it must be shared*" (1962, Thesis 4).

We might attribute to this thesis a still more global character if we escape the temptation to limit the meaning of "for us" exclusively to members of the Church, and regard the Son as the Second Adam, making His redemptive act available to the New Creation.

It is thanks to this correct perspective (referring the Church to Christ) that we were able to examine together the Word and the Sacraments. Initiated in 1957, this scrutiny was taken up again in 1962 (Thesis 7) where the emphasis was upon *the conjunction of the Word and the Sacrament* "which complement each other". What dominates and illuminates this analysis is this introductory affirmation: the mediation of Christ "becomes operative in the present in the symbols of the Word and the Sacraments" (1957, Thesis 3). Now this idea of a symbol, clearly distinguished "from a simple reminder of an event in past history, however necessary this may be" (*idem*) derives its validity and its depth of meaning from its relation to the mediation of Christ and of His sovereignty; He it is who, through the Holy Spirit, *makes them efficacious*.

These theses reveal, in a remarkably felicitous way, the intimate relation between the Word and the Sacrament; the comparison of our respective positions on this subject was very illuminating and led us to discover a synthesis. We should draw attention to the fact that this study still remains incomplete in so far as it could not be followed up with a fuller consideration of the necessity of both Word and Sacraments if we are to grasp the revelation of the Triune God, of the Incarnation of the Son and of the Indwelling of the Spirit.

This constant reference of the Church to Christ, which precludes the Church from thinking of herself as autonomous, puts us on our guard against the danger of an ecclesiology centred on the Church herself and not on her missionary nature. At this point, when one re-reads the theses, there emerges another impression, inseparable from the first.

2. Has this almost exclusive insistence on the relationship between Christ on the one hand, and the Church and its ministries on the other, resulted in a narrowing of our field of vision? Can we remain loyal to our original intention—that of discovering the root causes of our

differences—by following a single line, even though this line be of paramount importance? Certainly our method has developed over the years in a logical manner, we have relied upon it more and more while we considered problems as yet unsolved: the apostolic succession, the function of the ministers, their sacerdotal nature and whether this is distinct from the priesthood of believers. These were indeed unresolved, burning, contemporary problems; but the strictness with which we followed this single track, vital if our talks were not to end in nothing but words, might well have blinded us to a wider vision which would have enabled us to look afresh, from a new angle, at the problems which we did not succeed in resolving.

When a Protestant reads the theses for the first time, he is struck by the omission of doctrinal questions which seem fundamental to him if he is to explain his faith to Catholics, e.g. the doctrine of Grace, and the doctrine of the Kingdom of God. Other doctrines are barely touched on: the Person and Work of the Holy Spirit (without whom the doctrine of the Sacraments cannot be understood); the mission of the Church to the world. Doubtless, the fact that the 1955 session which was devoted to the relationship between Christ and the Holy Spirit did not produce any joint theses (any more than did the 1954 session on the Person of Christ) deepens this impression, an impression which still remains with those who took part in these earlier sessions.

Let us look in particular at the question of the Church's mission in the world, which is dealt with several times in our theses. From 1957 onwards, the central theme of the mediation of Christ is linked with mediation between God and men (Thesis 1), "the ministry of the Church is to bring *all men* into contact with this unique mediation" (Thesis 2) and this ministry sets the Church "in the service of men" (Thesis 3). "The universal mission which the Church derives from the mediation of Christ on behalf of the world" (Thesis 9) is here stressed. But the final emphasis brings us back to the action of the ministries in the Church and to the centrality of the Church's devotional life (Word and Sacraments).

In 1958, we had contemplated putting into the 1959 programme the question of the Church's authority; in fact we concentrated on authority within the Church, and were swayed by a conception which was based on the internal life of the Church, considered quite apart from her mission.

Similarly in 1960 the apostolicity of the Church was linked with the thought of "Christ offered to the world" (Thesis 6); the Church "is the Body of Him who, sent by the Father, in His turn sent the Church into the world". But, in fact, the transmissible element in the sending of the Apostles is described as a charge which is fulfilled within the Church: apostolic succession is conceived as being linked with the ministries which build up the Church. Doubtless this commission was received by the Apostles, but, as it were, as a consequence of their original commission: to proclaim the good news in the market-place, to be the ambassadors of Christ to the nations. Can we not see this commission being transmitted in the appearance, in the very centre of the life of the primitive Church, of the confessors and martyrs, whether they were ministers of the Church or not? If we interpret, as we have done, apostolicity as the building up of the Church and her loyalty to the faith as laid down by the Apostles, and the apostolic kerygma as cultic preaching and the witness of the Christian community, do we not turn the expression "sending into the world" into a mere expression, or at the very least give it far too narrow a significance?

Again, when we looked at the priestly nature of the ministry and of the faithful in our consideration of the sacerdotal activity of the Church (1962), did we sufficiently emphasize the thought that the Church is a priestly people existing for the sake of the world? If the Lord desires to have a priestly people on earth, is it not because He envisages her as called, not merely to the cultic activity of praise and intercession, but even more to the ministry of mediation between the world and God? Looked at from this angle, can we not speak of a "ministerial priesthood" of the whole Church?

While we express the view that our study has been too limited, too narrowly restricted to our internal Church life, this in no sense means that we are going back on what has already been made wonderfully clear, but that we are pointing out that certain intuitions have not been sufficiently developed and brought into the open. The question must also be asked whether the task of comparing our respective doctrines, so essential and, moreover, so beneficial when carried out in the setting of our conversations and our common search for the truth, does not have its limitations, of which we were made sharply aware in 1961. To overcome these limitations, must we not turn *together towards the world*, into which Christ sends all of us? Must we not be willing to accept a redirection in our thinking, a forsaking of our self-preoccupation, a "conversion" in the etymological and spiritual sense of the word, so that a new way of approach may be revealed to us, so that we may receive the vision of the full nature of the Church, as we realize that the service of man commits us more deeply to the service of Christ? That is my conviction. It is vital to underline the importance for the ecumenical dialogue of studying more profoundly certain suggestions which are scattered throughout our theses.

I do not intend to deal in detail with what was said about the Person and work of the Holy Spirit; however valid are the affirmations, interspersed in our theses, I feel that it is necessary in our future gatherings to return to the declarations of the 1955 session and to pursue this study of the Church and world in the light of the organic nature of the Trinity and of the individual. On the one hand, we shall see clearly the charismatic nature of the life of the Church and of the individual Christian; on the other hand, we shall be led to envisage the nature and mission of the Church and the existence of the world from the eschatological angle. "The goal of the Church is the Kingdom," we affirmed in 1957 (Thesis 10); this theme must be interpreted at a deeper level in a trinitarian perspective and with a charismatic and eschatological urgency.

Now that we can look at the entire collection of theses which represent seven years of ecumenical work, we are better able to see the omissions and the inadequacies. We might be able to add explanatory glosses which would enable us to avoid misconstructions. (Thus in 1958, Thesis 6, the expression "identified" with Christ is made clear by the context; "conformity" with Christ would be more exact, as we never become Christs! Similarly Thesis 6 of 1959 is so condensed that the idea of limitation is not clearly brought out; the minister is not the Lord Himself!) We discover tracks scarcely explored, questions left in suspense, still open. There are still unlit areas separating us, tensions amounting at times to opposition. And yet we can still say of this collection of theses what we said in 1957 of one particular point: "What still remains to be said . . . cannot invalidate what has been said."

Two final impressions are worthy of note:

At Presinge in 1958, although there is no record of this in the theses, we were led to ask ourselves this question: What is the nature of the authority of the ministries, bound up with the authority of Christ over the Church, the Head over the Body? Starting from the declaration of Christ (Matt. 28: 8–12) which describes the Church as a community *sui generis*, in contradistinction to a school, a family, or a state,

I had affirmed that what characterized the Christian Church was that all authority exercised therein should be of the same nature as the authority of Christ. Now we confess that *Christ is our Lord because He is our servant*, because He has given His life in our service. Only such an authority can deliver us from servitude to authorities which rule us by force or by law. In this way we speak in the Church of ministry and service, and the authority of this service is a reflection of the authority of the Servant-Lord. Any other authority based on rights or powers, changes the very nature of the Church. This interruption, made rather on the spur of the moment and perhaps in an aggressive manner, aroused serious opposition. Only one Catholic theologian had called the attention of his colleagues to this idea of service. That was in 1958 and it seems to be already quite remote now that this idea of service as the characteristic feature of ministry in the Church has played a leading part in the thought of the Second Vatican Council and in the *Schema, De Ecclesia*. So, at the breath of the Spirit, barriers which seemed unsurmountable may fall, reconciliations can create a new climate of thought in which fundamental oppositions may persist but tensions which prove to be false or superficial vanish.

The other memory is of something more recent, at Cormatin in 1962. Thesis 8 expressed the thought: "By giving Himself in the Eucharist to the Church, Christ draws her with Him in His own movement towards the Father." In classic Protestant thought Christ imparts Himself to the Church in the Eucharist and with His Person gives her the fruit of His sacrifice; there, in gratitude and as a fruit of faith, the Church offers herself as a living sacrifice, according to the magnificent phrase of Romans 12: 1. Suddenly, whilst I was listening to my Catholic brethren, a new intuition took hold of me: how can I offer myself as a sacrifice to God except through union with Christ who alone can draw me along this road of consecration and renunciation, how could I claim that I fulfil this act—and the Church with me —through my will to express my gratitude for the ineffable gift which has been bestowed on me, unless my will is inseparably joined to the will of Christ? The "all is grace" of the Reformers should not stop short at the movement of Christ towards His own, but should extend to the movement of the Church towards the Father. So, for me, one aspect of the Eucharist which I had not understood was made clear. This thesis, later drawn up in common, was for me a testimony of what I had received. Here again, although there are still opposing views on the sacrificial character of the Eucharist, barriers fell, a new fellowship in the faith appeared, and a new climate of thought and life made possible the drawing up of a new "joint thesis".

Will the reading of these theses make possible the discovery of that spiritual solidarity, which is the reward of the ecumenical dialogue, which saves it from being swallowed up in purely academic intellectual debates, which compels us to go forward along the road of a common search, which is at once costly and enriching? That is my desire in recalling these personal memories. These documents are undoubtedly the result of a theological method but, far more than that, they are the result of intercession, of a shared devotional life, and of spiritual flexibility. Such was the requirement of the founder of these gatherings, Father Paul Couturier: "Let theology be saturated with prayer."

HENRY BRUSTON, Lyon.

A CATHOLIC POINT OF VIEW

SEVERAL POINTS, essential to every ecumenical dialogue, seem to stand out from the "theses" drawn up in common over the last seven years. They concern the mediation of Christ, the priesthood of believers, the place of the Holy Spirit and eschatology. As we appreciate their great importance we shall be in a better position to understand the guidance they can give to other teams beside those who met in our gatherings at Les Dombes, Presinge and Taizé.

I. THE FUNDAMENTAL POINTS OF OUR AGREEMENT
(1) *Priority of the Mediation of Christ*

The mediation of Christ, implicit in the 1956 Theses on the state of original sin, which can only be adequately defined by reference to the salvation which Christ brings to us, occupies a truly central place in the 1957 Theses on the ministry of the Church. After the restatement in Thesis 1 of the normative text of 1 Tim. 2: 5, Thesis 2 is thus phrased: "*The ministry of the Church is to bring all men into contact with this unique mediation*. The mediation of Christ and the ministry of the Church are two inseparable aspects of the action through which God reaches us in Jesus Christ." Thus the ministry of the Church appears as serving the mediation of Christ; in this ministry the mediation of Christ keeps, manifests and unfolds its incontestable, constant and inceptive priority. Consequently, one can speak of the role of the Church as being "instrumental" and in a manner "sacramental". We shall come back to this point. The way lies open to a conception of the Church as the Body of Christ in which there is no danger of our losing sight of that clear distinction between Christ and the Church which overrules the union of Christ and the Church, and which our Protestant brethren often charge us with obscuring. Thesis 4 of 1958 is poised on an affirmation in which the priority of Christ is not compromised by His organic link with His Body which is the Church; on the contrary, her true relationship is expressed thus: "Jesus Christ is the Head of this Body, so that

71

the organic *unity* which He has with His Church does not affect His *lordship* over her. This *lordship* establishes a *distinction* which does not compromise the reality of the *union* of Bridegroom and Bride which exists between Christ and His Church."

This lordship of Christ equally makes possible the 1959 affirmations on pastoral authority. Thesis 1 declares this authority at the very outset: all the ministries are subject to it, and, pre-eminently, the ministry of authority. "Christ is the *sole Lord*," says this first Thesis, "Head and Judge of the Church. In consequence, no authority can exist in the Church except that which is founded on Him and constantly submitted to His judgment." The ministry of authority in the Church is entirely dependent on the mystery of the mediation of Christ, it is just one aspect of the service of Christ. The same principle operated in the same way the following year, when the *apostolicity* of the ministries was under discussion. "The charge transmitted by the Apostles is constantly accepted in the Church by the ministers whom *the Lord gives to His Body*. This transmission is *in the service of Christ alone* and offered to the world." This explains the seriousness of the difficulties encountered in 1961.

The principle which hitherto had ensured our unity seemed from this point to justify our disunity. The question at stake was whether or not the existence of the ministry in the Church implies a sacramental priesthood. The replies given by Catholics and Protestants, although contradictory to each other, sprang from the same source. "The difficulty which Protestants encounter in the Catholic position," it was stated in 1961, "arises *mainly* from the fact that this sacerdotal ministry appears to *obscure or to duplicate* both *the mediation of Christ* and the priesthood of believers. The difficulty which Catholics find in the Protestant position lies in the fact that *the true nature of the sacerdotal power of the unique Mediator is not made clearly manifest to His Body*." The disagreement arose from a common concern to safeguard the sovereign mediation of Christ. We were only able to get out of this impasse by starting afresh, in 1962, from what formed the basis of our agreement. Whatever activity the Church engages in, it is from Christ that the motive of this activity must derive. The first Thesis of 1962 reiterated, therefore, the principle which had always guided us and the wider implication which we drew from it: "*The unique character of the mediation of Christ, incarnate Son of God*, king and priest after the order of Melchizedek, does not imply His separation from men, but on the contrary, their recapitulation in Him who is Lord of the world and

Head of His Church." From that there flow a certain number of basic affirmations on the communicated mediation of Christ and on the priesthood of believers, of which we shall speak again.

Our common study had, therefore, its invariable axis in the mediation of Christ. If the mode of conceiving its manifestation within the Church divides us, the affirmation of the reality of this mediation in itself unites us. Further, when one is compelled to express everything in terms of this unique central truth, one discovers other gleams of light which join with it to form a kind of luminous outline. It is in this way that the increasingly clear recognition of the primordial role of the mediation of Christ became inseparable, in our view, from another affirmation which concerned the spiritual priesthood of believers.

(2) The Priesthood of Believers

The ministry which calls the Church to be the agent of Christ's mediation does not stop short at the Church but includes the world which is to be initiated, through her, into the mystery of Christ. Assuredly, the ministry finds its purpose in the Church in so far as through its agency the Church is to grow in Christ. However, the ministerial nature of the Church drives her outside herself so that the knowledge of Christ and life in Him may, through the action of the Church, become the experience of the world. Now knowledge of and life in the Mediator, communicated to the whole Church and which the whole Church in her turn must communicate to the world, is the spiritual priesthood vested in every Christian. In our conversations this priesthood was always considered as being at the heart of mission. "Without prejudging the question of the sacerdotal ministry, which is open to debate among us, *the universal mission which the Church derives from the mediation of Christ on behalf of the world* implies a priesthood of believers." How can there be any *compulsion* to speak of salvation without an *ability* to say, from the basis of personal initiation, what salvation means? Now, this initiation into salvation, which stamps the life of every Christian and on which his spiritual responsibilities towards the world are based, is indeed the priesthood of believers.

Almost in the same words, the same truth was stated in 1958, when the mystery of the Body of Christ was under consideration. In this Body the Head unites all its members to Himself and incorporates them spiritually with Himself, especially in the Eucharist. "In this unity," in the words of Thesis 6, "*Christ calls His Church to holiness. He confers this gift upon the Church by granting to each member to be in-*

corporated in Him and identified with Him in the Spirit." The spiritual priesthood consists of this identification of those who are incorporated in Christ with Christ Himself in accordance with the Holy Spirit, who unites us not only with Christ but organically one with another. This identification of those who are incorporated in Christ, with their Lord Himself, the same Thesis 6 of 1958 continues, "makes us members one of another and enables us to experience our proper relationship to Christ in our relationship to our brethren." The spiritual priesthood of believers permeates the life of the community and governs all person-to-person relationships. 1 Pet. 2: 5 states that the "living stones" are to be "built into a spiritual house." This house demands a quite specific ministry, which is not the only ministry but perhaps the most debatable of all: namely that of authority. After saying, at the end of Thesis 6 of 1958, that "the ministries have a special place in this twofold relationship" of the Christian with Christ, and of Christians amongst themselves, we had to remind ourselves in 1959, when speaking of the place of authority, which was the subject then under immediate consideration that it "is at the very heart of the fraternal relationships among the baptized," but adding forthwith "and at the same time transcends them," because of the very specific function of authority.

To define the properly hierarchical nature of this ministry of authority is still a difficult task. One can and one must, however, determine the line of conduct which should be followed by those who obey and by those who rule in such a way that due respect is paid to the fact that the baptized belong to Christ and that in consequence they exercise a spiritual priesthood. Thesis 6, ranging itself first with those who must yield obedience states: "*Obedience to the ministers must be offered as obedience to Jesus Christ the Lord; this safeguards Christian liberty,*" by safeguarding the proper dignity of those who belong to Christ alone (1 Cor. 3: 21-23). This dignity must be effectively respected by those who rule. This respect is only effectively demonstrated in so far as the baptized are treated as men who by their baptism have been initiated into the life of the Spirit, which is the essential mark of their spiritual priesthood. So Thesis 7 affirms: "Respect for the personality of the baptized entails for the one who exercises authority *the need, on their behalf, to be submissive to the Holy Spirit.*"

In the account which we gave in 1961 of our division over the matter of the sacerdotal priesthood, it appeared that the Protestants were fearful that the Catholic doctrine of the priesthood might "obscure or duplicate both the mediation of Christ *and the priesthood of believers.*" There can be no possible thought of this among Catholics. So we must recall at once our common agreement on this matter, as fundamental in our opinion as that of the mediation of Christ Himself from whom this priesthood derives. "Assuredly, we all admit that the Church is a sacerdotal body in the sense of 1 Pet. 2: 5 ff. For this reason, *whatever may be the answer that we have to give to the question raised by the ministerial priesthood, this can only be thought of as a function of the spiritual priesthood of believers* and as a function of the Christ-Church relationship," since it is on the Christ-Church relationship that ministerial priesthood is based. The spiritual priesthood of believers, as well as the mediation of Christ to the reality of which it is inseparably linked, is without doubt, in the very midst of our unsurmounted disagreements, an indisputable point.

In fact, in 1962, our common starting-point was the idea of the priesthood of believers. The first four theses describe the sacerdotal action of Christ in itself, while the remaining four describe its communication to the Church and within the Church, at least in the form of spiritual priesthood. The last thesis drawn up that year is very significant: "By giving Himself in the Eucharist to the Church, Christ draws her with Him in His own movement towards the Father, a movement of consecration and renunciation, of life in death. Thus He gives her a part in His own offering of praise to the Father and in His power to intercede for the salvation of the world. *In that way the Church, the Body of Christ, is revealed as being a sacerdotal people.*"

(3) *Place of the Holy Spirit and Eschatology*

The third subject on which we reached agreement was one the very nature of which compelled our unanimity: the work of the Holy Spirit and the eschatological horizon of the Church's life. Here I am putting together these two points into one: there is an intimate connection between the two. Indeed, the Church and eschatology are inseparable. For the Church, as the Body of Christ, is the work of the Spirit. Now the Spirit, breaking all the barriers of flesh and blood within which the history of men—and to a considerable degree the history of the Church—moves, bears the Church forward towards that appointed time when the profound truth of the Church will stand revealed. There is another consideration, on a lower level, which enables us to bring together these two points: we have not developed them as fully as we have developed the ideas of the mediation of Christ and the priesthood of believers. The subject of the Holy Spirit is, however, of paramount importance; to understand it we must strike out from the well-trodden theological tracks. In Protestant circles the thought of the Holy Spirit does not always evoke the Trinitarian overtones which ought to be heard. It suggests anthropology rather than authentic theology. Catholics often seem afraid to describe life in Christ in the terminology of the Spirit. Their vocabulary of "grace" is not always rightly integrated to a doctrine of the Holy Spirit. They would rather link this doctrine with Trinitarian indwelling (which they are rather apt to detach from its organic relation to the Incarnation) than to Christology properly so called. Catholic and Protestant failings on the subject of pneumatology, although they are complementary, are none the less real. Protestants, who maintain more firmly the relationship of the Holy Spirit to Christ, do not adequately reveal the Trinitarian depths of life in the Spirit. Catholics, who would be more directly aware of the Trinitarian significance of any reference to the Holy Spirit, often misunderstand the Christological implications of the revelations of the Spirit and of life in Him through lack of a precise vocabulary of "grace". That is why the references we have made in our joint theses to the place of the Holy Spirit are an expression more of a programme to be followed and a call to further study than a result achieved or a successful conclusion.

Thesis 10 (1956) on Justification reminds us that the response to God who saves us in Christ is made in the Holy Spirit. "*Under the action of the Holy Spirit* and in dependence on Him, man makes his own response to the initiative of God who justifies him in Jesus Christ, and so performs the works of God 'who worketh in us both to will and to do'." When, in 1958, we came to speak of the Church as the Body of Christ and to express "this living relationship of Christ to His Church" it was observed at once that it was Christ "who by His redemptive work has founded her", Christ who "*in the Spirit, gives her life, rules and guides her*" (Thesis 2). It is "*in the Spirit*" that Christ confers holiness on His Church "by granting to each member to be incorporated in Him and identified with Him" (Thesis 6). We have seen that it is this Spirit in the baptized which must be respected in the exercising of authority. As for the scriptural "deposit", which is the guiding light of the Church, this "can only be fully understood as it is experienced in the Church, *under the guidance of the Holy Spirit*" (1960, Thesis 5). The Holy Spirit, then, is He through whom our participation in Christ is made possible within the Church: "Christ is present now in His Church as the living Lord who has ascended into glory. He who was crucified is also He who is risen. *It is by participating in His living presence that we share, through the Holy Spirit, in the action by which He saves us"* (1962, Thesis 2).

Although precise, these indications are still modest. They point the road which has still to be travelled by both sides so that the meaning of Christ may take on its proper "pneumatism" and that pneumatology may give true depth to the meaning of Christ.[1] It is impossible to refrain from thinking what breadth of outlook on this subject we should gain from closer contact with the Orthodox Church. This contact raises definite problems of method, which we have discussed more than once and which are not easy to resolve. . . . Nevertheless, even if our ecumenical dialogue in the Les Dombes group is to remain primarily a dialogue between Catholics and Protestants, it must be deepened and extended, from Christology and ecclesiology into a true pneumatology. Everything points to the necessity for this. As yet we have achieved nothing concrete in this field. We must, however, stress two indications in 1957 and 1962 which might guide our steps.

In 1957, Thesis 10 stated: "The goal of the Church is the Kingdom, *the pledges of which are given to her*, as a kind of first-fruits of the completed act of mediation. For this reason the Church stands in relation to the Kingdom as something more than a transitory instrument." In 1958, Thesis 8 declared: "Authority in the Church has for its goal, not only to assemble and to organize the community, to direct it towards its missionary tasks, but also to prepare it for the time when the ministries will come to an end and the community *will be filled with the fulness of God.*" A more profound study on the Holy Spirit will surely enable us to define the Trinitarian depths on which the Church now stands and in which she will later fulfil her eternal purpose.

May one suggest, at the end of this brief analysis, a formula which sums up, from the Catholic viewpoint, our united achievements and which, we hope, will not shock our Protestant brethren, a formula which will make it easier for us to take a further step forward in our conversations—namely the definition of the Church as a Sacrament.[2]

[1] Cf. Dr. N. A. Nissiotis on the relation between the Spirit and life in Christ in the symposium *L'Esprit Saint*, Labor et Fides, Geneva, 1963, pp. 102–105.

[2] It is probably well known that the Constitution on the Liturgy promulgated by the Roman Catholic Church at the time of the second session of Vatican Council II includes a sacramental definition of the mystery of the Church. Although Father Congar frequently called attention in his *Blocnotes* of the Council (*Informations catholiques internationales*, 1963, Nos. 203, 205, 206) to the smooth transition from a juridical and formal conception of the Church to an ontological

II. DEFINITION OF THE CHURCH AS A SACRAMENT

1. The difficulties raised against such a way of defining the Church are far from negligible. Father Hamer has pointed out some of them.[1] One must, in fact, take great care, when speaking of the Church, not to separate the sign from the reality which is signified. If you describe the Church solely in symbolic terms, you ignore the fact that she is also the reality itself, which in another sense she serves. "In itself," writes Father Hamer, "the sacramental *schema* is illuminating. The mystical Body is at one and the same time an interior and an exterior reality. This inseparable duality can be best expressed by *sacramentum* and *res*. But, in this case, it must be insisted that the Church is composed of both. She is not simply the sacrament (the sign and the cause), but also the *res* (the reality signified and caused). Now when sacramental language is used without discernment, there is a danger of reducing ecclesiology to study of external elements."[2] The real risk of not fully understanding the sacramental definition of the Church ought not, however, to deprive us of the wealth of meaning it holds. It is certain that the *de Ecclesia* of Vatican Council II will use this sacramental language to describe the Church, as the *de Sacra Liturgia* has already done. This is a happy omen.

Judiciously applied to the Church, the use of this traditionally Augustinian vocabulary[3] is a very timely reminder that the Church in its institutional, hierarchical and "communal" visibleness possesses no value in herself and by herself; her validity consists solely in her rela-

and sacramental conception, this definition passed almost unnoticed. Canon Laurentin in his *Bilan de la deuxième session*, Paris, Le Seuil, 1964, does not mention it. This sacramentality of the Church is altogether different from the sacramentality of the Episcopate alone, which has been sufficiently emphasized. Inspired by a prayer from the Roman Missal for Holy Week, the Constitution on the Liturgy says: *Nam de latere Christi in cruce dormientis ortum est totius ecclesiae mirabile sacramentum*, Chap. 1, § 5. The French text of this Constitution may be found in *Documentation catholique*, Dec. 15, 1963, No. 1414, cols. 1636–1660. It is well known, too, that the *Schema* on the Church in its second revision contains two allusions to the sacramental nature of the Church. There is a reference to the definition of the Church as a sacrament by Fr. M. Gy in *La Maison-Dieu*, No. 77, *Commentaire complet de la Constitution conciliaire sur la liturgie*, Chap. 1, p. 22. I have analysed the work of the second session from the angle of the sacramentality of the Church in *L'horizon théologique de la deuxième session*, N.R.T., May 1964.

[1] *L'Eglise est une communion*, Paris, 1962, pp. 91–95.

[2] *Ibid.*, p. 92.

[3] N. M. Haring, *Berengar's Definitions of Sacramentum and their influence on medieval studies*, Toronto, 1948, pp. 109–146.

tionship to Christ, in whom, through whom and for whom she is the symbol. The spiritual reality of the Church (the *res* of the Augustinian analysis) is Christ in whom the Church grows in grace. This *res* establishes yet always transcends the value of the symbols. The definition of the Church as *sacrament* does not divorce the Church from Christ without whose action and impact she is nothing, nor does it identify the Church with any one of the seven sacraments, which would deprive them of their true meaning and would give only an approximate definition of the Church. On the contrary, the definition of the Church as sacrament brings us back to a basic, generic meaning which enables us to link the Church more closely with Christ.[1] One cannot push further a definition of sacramentalism which might justifiably disturb our Protestant brethren.

A sacramental definition of the Church need minimize neither the Word, nor the Scripture, nor the mediation of Christ in the Spirit. The way we adopted in the course of our gatherings at Les Dombes, Presinge, and Taizé, to explain our position on these matters in terms of sacraments properly so called, may clear up the problems which may be raised in a Protestant mind by the definition of the Church as a sacrament.

"Through the Sacrament," we said in Thesis 6 of 1957, "*Christ Himself* makes His mediation effectual in the Church, which rules out Donatism and magic. The sacraments are efficacious, not through the holiness of the ministry, not yet by the material significance of the rite but through the fact that they were instituted by Jesus Christ. Celebrated in accordance with His intention, *they are endowed by Him, in the Holy Spirit, with the promised efficacy. For this reason, the Word which points to the intention of the Mediator is fundamental to the constitution of the Sacrament in the Church.*"

Such a declaration can be repeated as it stands, whether one is speaking of the sacraments of the Church or of the Church as a sacrament. In fact, the sacramental nature of the Church rests not upon the assumed sanctity of her ministers nor upon the validity *per se* of her institutions; it is based solely on the fact that Christ, in the Spirit,

[1] M. J. Scheeben, *Le mystère de l'Eglise et de ses sacraments*, Introduction, translation, notes and appendices by Dom A. Kerkvoorde (*Unam Sanctam* 15), Paris, 1946. Henri de Lubac, *Méditation sur l'Eglise* (*Collection théologie*), Aubier 1953, 2 Chap. 6: *Le sacrement de Jesus-Christ*, pp. 125-203. Paul Evdokimov, *L'orthodoxie*, Delachaux et Niestlé, 1959, reference on p. 162 to Pseudo-Denys who calls the Church the sacrament of sacraments (*Teleton telete*) *Hier. Eccl.*, III, P.G. 3, 424c. Karl Rahner, *Kirche und Sacramente, questiones disputatae*, 10, Herder, Fribourg, 1960.

founded the Church to be the authorized minister of salvation. Far from conferring on the visible Church a kind of automatic validity, the nature of her foundation shows that she is absolutely linked to Christ, who establishes her to be merely the means for the transmission of His grace. The Church is fully aware of this. The authority she exercises in preaching the Gospel to men, in sanctifying them through the sacraments, in governing them as the People of God, does not exempt her from the sovereign authority of the Scripture and the Word, but rather demands an ever deepening fidelity to them. This is why what we wrote in 1962 on the Sacrament-Word relationship in the Church is still valid, now that we are trying to understand how the Church is herself the sacrament *par excellence*. "The power of Christ the Head," we then affirmed, "is fully exerted only in the conjunction of the Word and the Sacrament which complement each other. The Word leads to the Sacrament. The Sacrament makes the content of the Word come alive in a new way; the Word gives meaning to the Sacrament and guards it from error" (1962, Thesis 7). This living dialectic between Word and Sacrament retains its full validity when the Church is the sacrament in question. The sacramental definition of the Church cannot possibly exempt the Church from the standard of the Scripture and the Word. While she is not bound by the Word alone, the Church, as the total Sacrament of Christ, cannot dispense with Scripture or take its place. It is by the Scripture that she lives and tests her own life; the Scripture is her source of illumination and judgment. Thus the Sacrament which the Church is becomes the very place where the meaning of Scripture itself, normative on all matters, is tested and manifested.

It should suffice to suggest here that a definition of the Church as a sacrament does not surreptitiously reintroduce into the description of the Church a "sacramentalism" which is unacceptable when applied to the sacraments themselves. On the contrary, if we apply to the Church the richer understanding of the sacraments that we have discovered, we open new horizons to the ecumenical movement.

(2) *Ecumenical Significance of this Definition*

In the ecumenical field, as indeed in every other field, there is no spiritual road other than that which Christ Himself appoints in accordance with His own nature. It is only as we constantly seek our point of departure in Him, only as we submit ourselves constantly to Him, to the mystery of His Word, to His Scripture, to His Spirit and to

His life, that we can hope to be imbued with His will and His mind and to be in a position to rediscover in concert the visible identity of His Church. Instead of starting obstinately from our ecclesiological divisions over the *signum*, we must keep turning back to the content of the *res* where we shall be confronted with the demands, which we shall then understand, made by His symbol.

Such a road, one may surmise, does not involve the sacrifice of the visibility of the Church, but rather leads to a deeper respect for it. From what better source can we receive the Church than from Christ Himself? But some time must elapse before we can repair together to the same source to drink together of the same water with the same thirst. Ecumenicity, indeed, is this unanimous *movement*, prompted by the Spirit, of Christians towards their fountain-head, where they may receive not only Christ, through the life and hands of the Church, but also, in some way, may receive the Church herself from the very heart of Christ. We do well to speak of it as a movement. In fact, as Father Congar writes: "Ecumenicity is a movement: it is always in advance of itself. The Catholic Church solemnly and emphatically insists on her desire to follow the ecumenical road. But doubtless, few men suspect the increasing demands they will have to meet. Ecumenicity is not an easy road. It is an undertaking which requires patience. It will take generations before the roads blocked for so long can be slowly cleared, before positions which have hardened into a closed system of thought can become fluid and before that part of truth held by others can be accepted."[1]

In fact, certain Catholics would sometimes have us understand that they have already arrived, or more exactly that they feel no urge to start. Their doctrinal immobility passes in their eyes for the surest sign of the immutable truth they desire to serve. The only truly valid ecumenical action in their view is to insist, in season and out of season, whether it is relevant or not, on the primacy of Peter and his successors. The importance of this primacy is paramount, as is also the service which this primacy can and must contribute to world unity.[2] However, for the Church to be a visible symbol in all its fullness, room must be made not only for Peter and his successors but also for the Twelve and the episcopal Collegium. Room must also be made for fidelity to

[1] *Informations catholiques internationales* (206), Dec. 15, 1963, p. 1.

[2] See Y. M. Congar, *De la communion des Eglises à une ecclésiologie de l'Eglise universelle*, in *L'Episcopat et L'Eglise universelle* (*Unam Sanctam* 39), Paris, 1962, pp. 227-261.

Scripture, for the full sacramental life, for brotherly charity, for apostolic love for men, for the evangelization of the poor. To restrict the visible nature of the symbol to one single feature, however important this feature may be, without being equally concerned with the spiritual conditions which must be fulfilled before it can be clearly seen in its Christian radiance, means that we are betraying the symbol itself. The very word "symbol" presupposes that, through the medium of the symbol, the manifestation, one might almost say the *diaphanes*, of the *res* should be as complete as possible. For this reason, fidelity to Christ on one central point in the institution of the Church can never exempt us from fidelity to all the other points.

This requirement is equally valid for all the other communions. The essential element which is to be found in each of them, whether it be the Scripture or the idea of the Collegium, must be so lived out that the unifying purity of their Head may shine through it. As Prof. Evdokimov wrote: "The recognition of the real, therefore saving, presence of Christ in those with whom we are dealing is a condition of every ecumenical encounter."[1] If the attraction of the thought that Christ is present in each of the other communions is the *prerequisite* of ecumenicity, the first *demand* it makes is that each one shall grow to the fullest possible extent in the *reality* which his particular *symbol* bestows upon him. From this spiritual growth of Christ in each of us, from this increasing love offered by the members to their Head, sooner or later will emerge an irresistible passion for the visible unity of His Body. It is by loving Christ from within that fragment of the Church which is his own, that each can gradually discover that part of the Church which is missing in his love for Christ. In a word, out of spiritually renewed love for the *res* will spring the desire for a complete renewal of the symbol. On this basis, ecumenicity demands that everyone, starting from that part of the visible Church with which he is familiar, shall seek in mutual fidelity to Christ, to rediscover that part of the Church which is more or less foreign to him. This ecumenical approach is equally valid for Catholics. Involvement in the ecumenical movement does not require them to deny what they hold to be the full institutional nature of the symbol; it demands only that they abandon their narrowness, their errors and their complacency, and that they should practise the truth they profess by overcoming the prejudices which conceal it.

This, then, seems to be the true road to ecumenicity: starting from

---

[1] *L'Esprit Saint et la prière pour l'unité, Verbum Caro*, No. 55, 1960, p. 258.

the Church which we recognize as Christ's, we must seek constant spiritual encounter with Him in the belief that this living fidelity to Christ can ensure the discovery of the Church which we bring in question. This ecumenical road finds in the sacramentality of the Church in her relationship to Christ the doctrinal and spiritual blueprint of future developments. How can one possibly imagine that the Church as *symbol* will not directly benefit from the growing love shown by Christians to the *reality* of Christ which this Church signifies? Such a conception of ecumenicity, in any case, flows naturally from the kind of doctrinal reflection which was and still is our practice in the gatherings at Les Dombes, Presinge and Taizé. Our claim is not only that we approached ecclesiology in a spirit of Christological fidelity and compulsion, but also that we have always made it a rule to face each ecclesiological problem in terms of its Christological centre of gravity.

To some this method may seem too restrictive. Nevertheless it has enabled us to go forward. It is probable that it will enable us to make still further advances.

GUSTAVE MARTELET, Lyon-Fourvière.